Bards Annual 2022

The Annual Publication of the Bards Initiative

Bards Initiative

D1212083

James P. Wagner (Ishwa)—Editor, Compiler

Nick Hale—Submissions Editor, Compiler

Cover Art: Vincent (VinVulpis) Brancato

Layout Design: James P. Wagner (Ishwa)

Bards Annual 2022

Bards Initiative Staff:

James P. Wagner (Ishwa), Nick Hale, Jillian Wagner, Ryan Jones, Douglas G. Swezey, Margarette Wahl, Sharon Anderson, J R Turek

Dedicated to all Long Island Poets!

Foreword

Welcome to the 12th year of Bards Annual. This has been a very busy year, for poetry, and for everything else. Some people in this volume have been with us since the beginning, others are joining us for the first time, and some are sadly no longer with us. This volume contains poets of many different ages, backgrounds and beliefs. Poetry brings us all together.

Last year, we were launching the annual in sections again, but this year we are one big happy family again. We are very pleased to see far more poetry events coming back into the light again as some of the old venues have resumed operations and we even have some new ones.

Our book store, "The Dog-Eared Bard's Book Shop" has been open for a year now, and we've enjoyed many reading programs, book sales and of course, poetry readings in the new, wonderful space. We've enjoyed reading among old friends and making plenty of new ones! Poetry books from our publishing company sits on the tables in the store, and has found a new audience amongst the casual shopper. We've also recently restarted the poetry reading at Sachem Library and hope to keep it going strong as it had for years before Covid.

This is also going to be the 10th year for Bards Against Hunger, the program that was started here on Long Island, in 2013, and now has spread to more than 14 states throughout the country. We will be having plenty of local and national celebrations for this event as well.

So enjoy the poetry you hold in your hands. And let's look forward to the next year, with many more poetic opportunities to share.

~ James P. Wagner (Ishwa)

Table of Contents

Doug Abrams

Winter Onset

I watched as a full moon rose against a still-light sky,
      Drifting up through the last shredded clouds
      Of a passing storm.

Cold poured over my face in the dwindling light,
  Crows corkscrewed towards the fading horizon.
   Acute, the vastness of the park, the surface of the earth
    My specked markings a grain of sand on a grain of sand . . .

There is nowhere to turn in these moments,
  I am already there.
      In the bleakness of December landscape
      There is no voice echoes my thoughts.

      It snowed yesterday, and the ground is soft again.

Lloyd Abrams

predestined and inescapable

in my 1950s school days
i couldn't stand papier-mâché
nor the icky green bits in a&p's tomato sauce
nor the wet plastic vegetable bags
my mother washed and left hanging
on the inside grille of an aluminum screen door
so they shouldn't go to waste

if i'd fully grasped
what my mother had lived through
during her early years –
poverty
the spanish flu
the great war
the great depression –
and the enduring legacy
of an abusive alcoholic father
and a clinically depressed mother
who both escaped russia and poland
during the progroms –
then i might've had some inkling
what was motivating her
– what had triggered and sustained
her frugality and fear –
and at the very least
i could've cut her some slack

then it hit me
with a slap-on-my-forehead realization
that *i am* a second generation trauma survivor
– *not* of the holocaust
although that horror is *always*
in the back of our minds –
but of a dysfunctionally indigent existence
that transmogrified and relocated
from the powell street tenements in brooklyn
to an illusory and dreamlike
middle-class way of life
on suburban long island u s of a

as much as i try to elude
the victimized mindset
of the *shtetls* and ghettoes
of eastern europe
and of the hardships endured
in the unforgiving so-called *golden land*
i can neither override nor circumvent
the epigenetic changes
to my d n a

i have been bequeathed
my inheritance

Esther Alian

Adrift

A young girl stood at the river's banks,
Apprehensive of what lay beyond
The horizon in blue mist enshrouded.
Skin soft, lips rosy, eyes gleaming
Listening to its lapping calls
The youthful architect of an unfolding mystery.

Aboard a rickety vessel miles from shore
Tossed mercilessly by the restless sea
A woman raged at the gods,
Her hair fading, complexion weathered,
Rendered futile by the din of the heavens

If she could only return to that stable ground
She would forewarn the girl of the waters' treachery
Caution her to linger at the dock,
Or chart for her a safer course.

As lightning struck so too a flash of memory
Of days lived and gone
Nights passed in bliss and in agony
As the seas, calm and rough,
Beckon the girl,
And she knows, her heart shattering, it is she.

Sharon Anderson

Picture This

Procyon, Sirius, Betelgeuse
glow in the winter sky,
twinkle like beacons,
form a nearly perfect triangle.

Cloud formations fascinate me.
I lie in the grass, stare up,
find angel and puppy shapes,
flowers and fluffy birds.

Those who study stars
seek formations too; stare up,
find Orion, Libra,
all manner of fish and fowl.

My cloud paintings dissipate
almost immediately,
shift from rabbit to rubble
even as I watch.

Star formations, however,
live on forever,
or at least for the time
we humans know as *forever*.

Fantasizing as I gaze upward,
I ponder my shifting clouds and wonder,
will Orion's belt one day unfurl?
Will Libra's scales become unbalanced?

Will anyone be alive to see it happen?

William H. Balzac

Intercession

Tonight, and every night
I try to express,
As best I can,
Our mode of Prayer
For Others:
Within lines,
And between lines...

With Stanzas
As rich as Hope,
As any flying Dove
Which may have been spotted
Above scarred and battered lands
Or
In trains bound
For a neighboring border,
Which had witnessed these
Movements,
Not too long ago
In the Grand March
Of Time.

There is illness still,
In minds
And Bodies,
When prayer is lifted
Like a rope in a Church steeple;

7

Like bells rung in a Calling,
Amongst Funeral processions,
Of friends
And Family,

When this Intercession
For Others,
Touches all,
And my simple Prayer
In the last Stanza,
Is the fullness of Faith:

Poem,
For those
So much like myself...
But, Other,
Just like me:
Forever Abiding,
Love.

Christine A. Barbour

A Mermaid's Tale

I feel her. Feel her brush my legs with her tiny fins;
and her beautiful tail is the color of aquamarine.
Her body is made of sequins; and the foamy sea that
surrounds her are tiny bubbles that swim around my feet.

Her hair is like cornsilk, almost clear, as it waves
out behind her with the ocean's rhythm and lifts her
up on the sand of a salty sea.

Will I ever feel this way again – stepping into
a summer's wave? My toes are weightless,
drowning in the sand: appearing, disappearing.
My heart beats with hers. Was she here?
Did I feel her or was she
simply seaweed?

Jess Beck

The Review

I met a bookstore in the winter
And another in the spring
A guest in the snow
Stubborn weed in the flowers

Aisles are mountains
Up on tiptoes, peering over
Fell straight down into a smile

Two bookstores and another
Pencil   markings on the inner cover
With the damp vanilla smell of fresh paper
And all that I remember
A face buried in a shoulder

Tracing fingers along   the spine
Rubbing pages between the lines
Thin as the skin stretched across the hand
I brushed as I walked by

What was the inventory on mystery this time?
On some adventure I was chasing
A weathered statue anchored to the checkout line
First edition faces reflecting the glass casing

What was the inventory on romance this time?
In the moment finding poems between our teeth
Back pressed hard against library carts
And will it be that long until they meet?

Falling in love at a bookstore,
When your walls come down
Your stories will live in the pages on the shelves
I wouldn't recommend it

Falling in love with a bookstore,
Your stories will die with the shelves
When the walls come down

And I wouldn't recommend it

Antonio Bellia (Madly Loved)

Desire

A wish is static
Stagnant
Eventually putrid

Desire is dynamic,
Moves, ignites
Sets the senses
On fire.

Passion is
The blood
Thought the breath
Of life.

It all burns
Day and Night
Brightly and clearly,
Illuminating
The Vision..

The walls of
Limits crumble
Guards of the
Impossible faint

Veils of the
Invisible tear.
The abstract
Crystalizes.

The created has
Become the creator.

Robyn Bellospirito

Autumn Balloon

I am the child-less
I am the free spirit
I am the harmless
I am the lonely ghost
I am the whirling dervish
I am the soul sister
I am the down dragger
(the drowned dagger).
Afraid to fly, not want to die,
scared to live,
sad to run
for my life.
peace-full
dis-tract
jam-packed
jump-track.
Bow ties
and false lies
and free flies
and buoyant cries
never goodbye
never deep fried
just tongue-tied.
Set free
upon the wind
like an autumn
birthday balloon.

Damien Bettinger

Recognized by the light of one's own kind

Undreamt interruptions

overwhelming emotions

exploring the explorations
with in these...

lucid, therapeutic, dream state curations.

processed by what's been made conscious,
Living amongst the newly developed
sensory-memorial context, of our ability, to put this concept, into perspec-
tive...

These examples could very well be the same faculties that determine the rate
of our own interpersonal growth and change.

exercise the star parts
Bursting from one's...
darkened heart...

set something on fire with them!

imagine one thing coming from nothing...

over and over again...

these places, with these characters,
playable or not,
live infinitely complex lives
with subtle differences
that can only be recognized
after a practical application has been put into practice.

Danger keeps deaths most restful design,
at peace with what ever happens to the mind.

We wonder what we can do to improve...

the self
and all else
that would other wise be
left behind

"Recognized by the light of one's own kind"

Reyna Vasquez Bisono

I Don't Write Love Poems

I Don't Write Love Poems-
but bring me sunflower sunsets
as I pray for Love letter symphonies
and
sing me makeshift melodies
that make me dream of
butterfly quartets
beneath my ribcage,
Chaos futtering with every breath
I dare you to make me lose.

I Don't Write Love Poems-
but make me lose my mind
and maybe I'll write about you.

John A. Brennan

The Meadow Ballet

The old man could handle a scythe.
Could swing it with the easy grace of a matador in a bullring in
Barcelona. Could turn and pivot, sure of foot, like a lithe ballerina
on the stage at the Bolshoi.

The grass, defeated with surgical precision, fell in complete surrender
prostrate beneath him, each cut a perfect arc of knowing the way.
He would spit on his palms, grasp the handles surely, but lightly.
Glints of sunlight would flash like mirrored signals with each slice.
The steel, sharp as obsidian, mowed with near silent swish.

Wielded like a gladius before the barbaric grasses, he made the
meadowlark and linnet flee in frightful flight before him, feathers
ruffled. The field-mice scurried helter-skelter, squealing for mercy.
And always at full stretch, that graceful swing, that perfect step,
the meadow ballet.

The stone, nestled in the back pocket, waited it's turn.

He would pause, straighten his back and stand the scythe on end,
dulled blade pointed at the earth. Would wipe the sweat from his
brow with the back of his hand, slide the stone along its length and
up the other side. Hone with an angle of perfect degree, steady, sure.
The reaper's shadow, long and black, lay outstretched on the stubble
behind him. Would drink deeply from the can of milk, and then,
the second act.

Laurel Brett

Summer, 1990: Jones Beach
Early Morning

6 a.m.
Jones Beach.
The beach is empty
except for us and the gulls.

David, in his Buddha posture,
is not yet one,
and Mark holds him
out to the world, ankles crossed.

Mia runs ahead,
her heart
echoes the beat of the surf,
her auburn tendrils blaze red.

In the distance
early launched boats
dot a horizon
like you'd see in a painting.

Mia laughs, she giggles.
She opens herself
to the sun-bright blue of sky and sea
like the sails on the tiny distant boats
open themselves to the wind.

Richard Bronson

Shooting it Up

They'd met at a Dallas gun show –
muscle bound ex-Navy SEAL,
a gun salesman now,
automatic weapons his specialty.
She was there to buy a Glock.

Fortyish, dirty blond, divorced,
"You know how it is," she told me,
sitting in my office. "He asked me to dinner,
and both a little drunk, we went to his place."

Next day, she flew back home,
promised to return –
then back and forth each weekend,
hot and fast for a month.

She'd wanted a baby, so desperate
to conceive. "Find a way,"
he'd said. "I'll send you my jizz!"

Smiling coyly, she opened her handbag,
handed me a plastic cup. "I found a kit on *Amazon*
to FedEx his sperm, but months have passed and nothing.
This time around, I thought you'd better check him out."

I placed a drop on a slide, took a look.
"I'm so sorry, no sperm there," shaking my head.

"Wish I could say something different.
Those bulging muscles are the clue.
He's a testosterone user
shooting often, but shooting blanks!"

Carlo Frank Calo

The concert at Tanner Park – July 2017

We got there early and set up our blanket and chairs on the grass
Overlooking the bay and the bandstand, the two of us sipping a beer and
then,
Arriving for the concert, a group of six came and sat a bit too close,
And skootching to my right, I give us all some space
But the distance between us increased to infinity as they continue to sit,
oblivious,
While we all stand for the Anthem, yet they talked and sat and laughed
through its' playing, ignoring the words,
The words which spoke of their freedom, spoke of their freedom to do just
that,
And being too self-absorbed to respect what was happening, they totally
missed the point.

Lee grace Cannella

Thursday Afternoon

Thursday arrives
whispering:
you will see
what they will bring
when they come in
one by one...

I never know what Thursday brings,
I only know it is special.

They wait for me
as I climb the steps
to the third floor.

The blind man,
tapping his cane
against the wall,
finds his way to the class.

Others come in slowly...
pushing wheelchairs
and walkers.

Wearing words in their eyes
and life on their lips.

The circle forms,
the litany begins.

The room is filled with sound:
thoughts...memories
sorrows...griefs...tears…
smiles...laughter…
gratitude...acceptance.

On Thursday afternoon
I learn that I am blessed.

I become a living poem
written by a gracious pen.

Shannon Cardinuto

Darkness

The further down, the deeper she falls into the darkness of it all.
It feeds on the souls of those she loved most;
you led her to believe she was the one. Now she is a ghost.
Deeper and deeper she falls into the darkness of it all.
With your selfishness, she decays under the ground where generations will
play.
Perished and forgotten, as if she didn't matter.
With her death, she thought the memories would shatter.
Instead, all they do is chatter.
Chattering about the love that she lost,
Reminding her for eternity what that love cost.
Deeper in to the darkness she falls wanting to hear nothing of it all.
But when she begs the chatter to stop,
They laugh and mock her until she drops.
Deeper and deeper into the darkness she falls
screaming and pleading down the halls, begging and crying to only be heard,
so the chatter can stop, so it will just be her word.
Deeper and deeper into the darkness she falls
her word against his against them all.
She will have her day,
she will have her final say.
Deeper and deeper into the darkness she falls
he will know she loved him through it all.
Much after as she begged him not to go,
even though he chose another,
he came back for the show.
As she's handed that final blow,

the further down the deeper she falls.
Screaming through the night
his name she would call,
deeper and deep as she falls.

Cate Chirico

Visual Purple

It is said that there are
two hundred Kuri in existence ,
thin slicing in rapid cognition,
narrow slices of experience ,
automated accelerators navigating
the field of pure potential .
Immortal inner dweller weaving
Akashic moss code with
gossamer threads, release me
just enough to sleep .

Abandoned abolished prophets dismissed by mad desire,
you who surrendered your peace
to the Periwinkle and the Hawthorne
Oh light fingered one ,flower picker,
take me by the hand , move the shadows of the sheltering sky ,
allow me to lie half asleep behind
the altar of your smile .

City on top of city , Palestine
Lebanon, Syria ,Turkey
where Tellos abound ,
tell-tale broken pottery stored
the grain and the wine
and then the almighty coin .
Bring out the new treasures
The book and the spade

Layer upon layer
City upon city
Coin upon coin
Ah and then comes the oil!
Cherished anger
Unforgiving spirit
Fast from toxic thought,
starve the bitterness, starve the pretense ,fill up with redemption wisdom ,
sanctification ,
you're one Jesus away from heaven one Mohammed away from hell .

Anne Cognato

In the Rain

The world turns gray in the rain,
Warm drops land on my eyelashes
Then I brush them away

Birds perched on wires
Like musical notes
Getting wet

When you were little
We splashed in the puddles
and danced in the rain.

I wonder
where the birds sat
before there were power lines.

Anne Coen

Keep Moving

Forget what you've learned
about the shortest distance between two points
or the way a crow flies.

No oracle will guide you,
though even a crudely drawn map with indiscernible landmarks
would be preferable to having no directions at all.

Wear comfortable shoes.
Be aware estimated arrival times are subject to change without notice.
Keep moving.

Your route consists of roads less traveled
through trash-strewn alleys and vacant lots littered with broken glass.
Keep moving.

On lucky days you may encounter welcome distractions:
sunny vistas of charming coastal towns, purple-hued mountain meadows.
But you know you can't stay.
Keep moving.

Mostly you will feel like a solitary traveler
stumbling towards Mount Doom in the desolate land of Mordor.
Keep moving.

Become familiar with the silent companions who have always been by your
side:

Pain has been polishing your imperfections into gems of compassion.
Gratitude has been gifting you with bouquets of simple victories.

As you keep moving you'll discover
your feet have grown wings
ready to fly you home.

Marty Cohen

Late In The Game

He looks the runner back to first and deals.
With runners on you have to have a plan.
The game goes on no matter how you feel.

Talent and speed go just so far. Real
Pitching starts with a sore and tired arm. A glance
Looking the runner back to first, he deals.

How he got on doesn't matter. You have to deal
With the contingency, the runner's dance.
The game goes on no matter how you feel.

The runner's looking for the sign to steal,
Green light from the bench to take a chance.
The pitcher looks the runner back and deals.

The runner isn't going, rocks back on his heels.
The batter shifts his weight, adjusts his stance.
The game goes on no matter how they feel.

The infield comes alive. The fans peel
From their seats, aswarm with cheers and chants.
The pitcher looks the runner back to first and deals.
The game goes on no matter how we feel.

Jamie Ann Colangelo

Homage to a Task

By Jamie Ann Colangelo

I thought about a task
the one I hate the most
it's not done everyday
biweekly at the most

I strip all the bed sheets
and put them in the wash
dust all the furniture
and mop the dirty floor

The sheets are set to dry
the bedroom is put back
the bed is freshly made
and beckons me to sleep

Ed Coletti

Every song's got more to it

That's what smacked me down
watching the documentary
I CALLED HIM MORGAN
It continued to gnaw at me
that in a poem I'd been so unfair
to Helen because she'd shot Lee Morgan
that transcendent trumpeter to death

Helen Morgan down South
who bore her first child at 13
her second at 14 and who gave
both of them up to be raised
by their grandparents before
she married a much older man
who drowned and she again was
alone but now independent and

On her way to New York City
where she earned her living as
a phone answering service worker
to keep an apartment on 53d St
where she cooked and made home
for herself and half the jazz musicians
in New York who knew her as their Mom
who knew how to cook and care for them

Not the least of these young Lee Morgan
she pulled from the gutter of heroin
took him to Bellevue started him on methadone
and a new life clean and brilliant as the best
horn player of his very young generation

Lots of love between them though Helen
quite understandably had an impossible time
abiding Morgan's vibe for a woman who he called
his friend and who also understood him the way
Helen Morgan did   Two women who understand
one man too well   The first would never abide
the latter   As with Frankie and Johnny it had to end.

And boy could that Helen ever cook!

Lorraine Conlin

Staying at Grandma's

I remember sleeping over Grandma's house,
helping her with chores after Grandpa left her
for reasons I didn't know back then and didn't care,
because I loved being alone with her.

She taught me how to shake off the dirt
clinging to carrots, potatoes and beets,
pick ripe string beans and cucumbers off the vines.

Azure summer skies peeked through towers of corn,
their husks brushed my bare skin giving me goose bumps
as Grandma and I walked through the maze.

Grandma let me collect the speckled eggs from hay-lined coops,
chicks and hens at our heels, pecking and clucking.
I'd place them ever so gently in the basket she created
by twisting her hands around the tattered hem of her apron.

In the house Grandma nestled the eggs
between the beans and greens in a silver colander.
She'd gather her apron around the soil-laden vegetables on the counter,
spill them into the sink to soak.

She'd wash and dry her hands,
pour milk into my favorite glass,
slice homemade shortcake,
cover it with slivers of strawberries

and fresh whipped cream
she made before I woke up
and joined her in the garden.

Jane Connelly

Burning Embers

Each night after work we'd head out the door to
Bowling alleys, diners and *The Triangle Rest* –
Kicking up sawdust on the old dance floor, while
The voice of Johnny Cash crooned we were *Hotter than
A Pepper Sprout*, and *Sunday Morning was Coming Down*.
We threw our heads back and laughed when ghostlike
My mother would appear in her nightgown proclaiming
We'd all be hags by the age of 30, while we sat
Around the kitchen table guzzling the last sweet drops
Of our amber tea, squawking through the wee hours
Planning the fun we'd have next, and next, and next...
Time itself was *Old and in the Way*, shuffling near,
But out of sight – and we paid him no mind.
Now, more than twice that age, I sit at
The same wooden table, with failing eyesight
That *Makes My Brown Eyes Blue*; and ears
No longer able to grasp the words of songs of
Momma, lost loves, or *Happy Trails*; now
Riding into a golden sunset with missing teeth
Like some *Coal Miner's Daughter*, with skin
Crinkled from the *Prairie Wind* of life; surrounded by
Sounds of Silence but for the *Lonesome Dove* cooing
As I do my *PJ Shuffle*, a sidestep to the beckoning couch
To dream of the joys of burning my candle at both ends
Back when I was *Forever Young* and free.

Ushiku Crisafulli

I Write for You
(dedicated to Graham Halsey)

You wrote for the page,
I write for the stage.
Now I write for you.

You'd write for the love,
I write for acclaim.
Now I write for you.

You'd write all the wrongs,
I make right through song…
and I'll write for you.

You'd write for emotion, the truth, and the feeling,
These days I barely write, and spend even less reading…
but I write for you.

We met both as writers and fans of Pip,
now I write for the cheers when I fuckin' spit sick.
But fuck all that shit, now I write for you.

If I could pen a new ending
I would rip up the script.
Cos right now just ain't right, and your writing is sick.

Michele Cuomo

Long Island Railroad: 1992

You weep-the diesel car rocks you to sleep
Bay Shore bound, your SoHo lover untrue
raw cold, chapped, & weak, the learning curve steep
that wait at Jamaica station-- broke you
Streaked cheeks ragged, unsated, unmoored
black snow and hole in boot and frozen salt
then you remember that moment you soared
above the bridge and tunnel platelet fault
You can remember that moment you roared
like that polar bear in the Central Park zoo
now back to this moment, dreaded, abhorred
eyes open now, the rest of you is too
In years to come you'll reflect on this pain
& smile, 'cause you got yourself off that train

Paula Curci

That Morning When She Was Fifty-Eight

That morning when she was fifty-eight
she slept a little late.
The oatmeal stewed,
The coffee brewed.
It was a day like no other.

Back when she was twenty-eight
she simply accepted her fate.
Not by design.
It all turned out fine,
even with days of squander.

In the afternoon, of her fifty-eighth,
she felt her weight.
The lines on her face.
Her slower pace,
and a saddened sense grew from wonder.

On that night, when she was fifty-eight
She couldn't wait
to make a wish and blow
and although, she'd settle in to crow
she wished for fifty more years to ponder.

Samantha Curra

The Bridge
(Dedicated to my sister)

The gap of dry muddy time
Has been my friend during the drought
The vacant holes inside my mind

I've always been a decade behind
Empty spaces filled with doubt
The gap of dry muddy time

Puzzle pieces are hard to find
When they are lost or thrown out
The vacant holes inside my mind

I'm learning how to build and bind
The memories I've lived without
The gap of dry muddy time

I don't regret what's yours or mine
It's something I've stopped thinking about
The vacant holes inside my mind

I've built a bridge to cross and climb
I no longer fear the drought
The gap of dry muddy time
The vacant holes inside my mind

Jackie Dawn

unfinished symphony

pressed to the glass
this fish tank
settles in four shades of onyx
and i look for the light.

here, i stand
on the precipice of seasons,
and listen to the other things
breathing
wheezing
seething
and singing
a tiny unfinished symphony
a cacophony in my ears

a stroll of spiders along the frame
like a palm against the curve of skin
while secrets skitter between leaves
and the moon winks over us

here on this precipice
panes fall away
as heads fall back
i am alight this night
and i wonder
what time it is in your sky.

Max Dawson

Grandfather Clock

Oh mighty Grandfather Clock, how you stand so proud and tall
      Bold and solitary do you dwell in the hall
Like a cathedral do you stoically stand, your only movement is your pendulum, your small and big hand
Under the sun's golden rays, under the moon's bright white gaze, during rain and during snow, you announce the day and night's times
Like an angel you sing the Westminster Chimes
Your song like seraphim drifts through the house, through hallways and rooms and into the den
Quite perfectly do you imitate the speech of Big Ben
Your melody soars through the house like Big Ben's chimes soar above London's streets and
towers
As you chime all twenty-four hours
But hush, look at the time, let us listen to the Grandfather Clock Chime

Jeanne D'Brant

Plague Lament 2021

A door closes tightly and locks
TSA, LGA, JFK now extinct to possibility
The leaden skies are New York nasty
Take-offs to the brilliant blue on hold

Oh, to be in the Caribbean
Accents lilting, drifting on a breeze
Sweetly syllabic musical patois
Caribbean is verboten

Oh, to be in Morocco
Steaming tagines of plum and spice
Medinas, markets, mesmerizing madness
Morocco is forbidden

Las Islas Canarias must wait
While Patagonia's summer sun melts the high icy passes
And passes me, in isolation, on by
No Pacifica, vanished Rapa Nui and the moai,
A tear wells in my eye

Passport silently scowls, gathering dust motes instead of stamps
suitcases sit on silent wheels empty of anticipation
I make Siri an Irish lass, ears keen for alternative accents
While Alexa stalwartly plays on in the midwinter gloom

Silken cords of home entrap my ankles
Chop wood, carry water
Haul wood, carry on
Blessed are we who live by the fire amidst discord and disease

India DeCarmine

Poolscape with the Drowned Ophelia

We've been shown
 the old masters understood.
No matter that you're fair, or
mad, or good,
no matter that you fly, or fall,
or drown,
ships will sail on, and
ploughmen will plough.

A splash,
A feather,
Paint them together;
A song,
A willow,
Ophelia's billow
(being her garments that held
her aloft,
until they didn't - though
drowning was soft.)
Notice the pool with said
willow aslant.
But try to stop for her death.
You can't.
Diver and heron in
 commensurate arc.
But not in sympathy.
No dogs bark.

Debbie De Louise

Knight In Shining Armor

A blue wind blows from the north.
Medieval trees sway
casting shadows across the courtyard.
A magical flue plays
tinkling a tune to summon my lover.

He comes to me on a white horse
charging into my dream like silver lightning.
So bold,
So strong,
My knight in shining armor!

He carries me to his castle
where we sip from silver goblets
the dragon's nectar.

He lowers the drawbridge of my heart
and daringly plunges into the moat below.

We fall asleep before the fire,
his silken head between my breasts.
Outside, the thunder roars,
but in my dream, I'm safe, secure.
He's beside me,
within me.
My knight in shining armor!

The fire's ashes burn themselves to dust.
The single wine glass lies empty,
the remains of its amber liquid
impotent poison in the morning light.

I awake alone,
not lonely
for the memory of the fantasy
fulfills me,
sustains me.
My knight in shining armor!.

Ben Diamond

On The Death of Carroll Sockwell

An ornate picture frame with nothing in it.
Down the block a topless bar, many nights
In poverty. He slept on steamer trunks.
He barely drinking, just like that.
No one ever knows the price of gin.
He would arrive at your party, drink himself dizzy and
Pee in your closet.

Camels with thundering muskets -
A landscape of fiery reds and black.
The truth, he said, is obscurity and timid yellows.
The more drinking.
Just like that.
Shapes appear, black on a blacker genre
That the ignorant famously dismiss.

He blubbered something about Arabs,
Landscapes of fiery red,
Obscurity and timid yellows.
A creek bed hurtled toward him
Like an ornate picture frame;
The topless bar, the steamer trunks, the drinking -
No one ever knows.

Michael E Dilgen

Lonely Addiction

You take a sip of loneliness,
a cursed and bitter dose,
Then wash it down with apathy
toward the ones you love the most,…

You drink until you see their ghosts
as you slur and accuse the past,
Then stagger away from the moment,
a moment never meant to last,…

Spirits from the heavy glass linger in your mind,
Terrified by what you feel
and the feelings you still can't find,…

All of this is sobering
yet you always come back for more,
Sorrow now,
your lonely addiction,
letting go the only cure,…

Michael Duff

Where's Sharon?

Where's Sharon?
I say it to myself.
Where's Sharon?
I say it to her daughter when I think she knows:
Where's Sharon?
She feigns exhaustion and sighs.
I say it to her sisters and her mother,
and her brother when her brother is in from California.
Her other brother from California, I haven't met yet, but when I do, I'm sure
I'll ask him:
Where's Sharon?
I ask her nephew who lives with her:
Where's Sharon?
He points with his chin and smiles.
(I like that he smiles.)
I ask her other nephew:
Where's Sharon?
He pauses and looks right and left, as in confusion.
Then, his girlfriend gives him a push,
and says, Oh, Henry!
Sharon turns out to be just outside my line of sight.
I, behind a pilar or a relative, say again,
Where's Sharon?
So, he grumbles and calls: Sharon!

Sometimes, I'm a long way away
and I think:

Where's Sharon?
I know she's not there.
I know she's far away.
But my heart has its own eyes, and looks upon itself,
and there's Sharon.

Peter V. Dugan

Avant-garde Café Bards

Post-mod poets unveil a wired vat anthem
of misnomer ear candy epaulets
filled with alien slang sarcasm,
a melodrama of cynicism and hedonism,
as they wield their pens like rapiers
in the hands of swordsmen
slashing, stabbing, hacking and slicing
through the jungle and jumble
resonant in the mediocrity
of middle-class life.

At night, you can hear them howl,
creating a cacophony
of natural and unnatural sounds
flowing into the jazz like euphony
of existence, with words
that are raw, flawed and unpolished.

A primal scream, a rap on life,
a static noise that echoes
eloquent, powerful words
ready to burst into a spectrum of colors,
images and stories
painted in the pastels of nature
and imagination.

Madelyn Edelson

The View From 90

A dozen robins littered the lawn, deftly pulling worms,
Claiming their brief moment on life's ever-shifting stage,
While noisy jays and brilliant cardinals swooped in
To sweep the smaller birds away.

Ninety springs have come and gone today.
The crowd is thinning as I write.
Dear friends and colleagues fade into the shadows.
I call them back to jolt my memories.
The laughter and the tears are juxtaposed in shards of years.

Having tasted agony and ecstasy and borne the dregs
I am restless and dissatisfied.
Loss of a brother, children's births, line up, jostle one another.
"Pick me," each memory insists.
"Bring me back to front and center. Bring me back to life!"

Daddy lifts me to his shoulders, pushes through the storm,
Then retreats with his broad grin into his waiting picture frame.
Mother, in her portrait on the stair,
Absent the pain of later years, smiles wistfully.
A son's loss will fracture that sweet smile, leave her permanently gone.

Today as every day, I slip on four precious pearls,
Each gem so distinctive, each facet blazing signs of worth.
The oldest pearl went forth into the world to prove her highly polished
skills,

The next, nudging the elder, raced to catch up, spreading trinkets in her wake.
The third, armed with protective gear, became the keystone of her string,
Pulling the others into a straight, productive chain,
While the fourth, like Peter Pan, danced bravely on a limb,
But couldn't hide her all too sensitively offered skin.

Drops of water hang suspended from the paddle
As it rests athwart the gunwales of the old canoe,
Each drop a distillation of a treasured time
Extracted from an album stored within my mind:
The outracing of a summer storm, pulling fiercely at the oars;
Four bodies shaking my bed as lightning flashed and thunder roared.
Brownies laced with pot, brought by a troubled teen;
The moon walk only conceived as we madly twisted rabbit ears,
An incantation to the gods to clear the TV screen!
Today grandchildren armed with phones idle on the porch
Spinning daydreams spun by parents years before.

The weary world spins off its axis, out of all control.
Troops are mustered, missiles whine, targeting civilian homes.
Pandemic wounds fester in those reeling from the far-flung assault.
A hidden enemy exacts a harsh extended toll.
The politicians wrangle late into the night
While a divided country shreds all decency.

But when I am engulfed by life's deepest despair,
I reach into my store of memories and dust off one, so rare.
Two solitudes that brushed against each other,
Settled on a loaded magnetic field to face the world as one.

Murmurations of returning starlings hang suspended in the dawn
Then settle as a blanket on the lawn.

The sweet smell of newly mown grass rises in the air, defying age, embracing memory,
Trumpeting triumphant notes of spring, of new life, of treasured moments held and passed
To outstretched arms poised to accept the burden of my thoughts, the continuity of love.

Alex Edwards-Bourdrez

Uncertain Belonging

We came upon a gang of geese,
interlopers along the docks,

hanging out, cool, in shiny black
and chestnut brown, checking us out.

It was the leader, I suppose,
who twitched, then, slow as grace can be,

imperious, cleared the bulkhead,
then floated there, beyond our reach—

a nature-bestowed privilege
the others claimed, as well, in turn,

except one, whose hesitancy,
familiar, claimed my empathy.

Lynn B. Elfe

Everything Will Be Alright

Always have what you have,
And enjoy the full impact.
Accept your limitations and strengths.
They are yours, as a matter of fact.

Everything will be alright.
Let tomorrow graciously show,
The power that is within you.
Let your ardent energy radiate and glow.

Experience each day in your balanced stride.
Look quietly towards the sky with delight.
The sun will find its way through the clouds,
And you will again,
have an opportunity,
to make a day take flight.

Make sure you live one day at a time.
Be in this moment without regret.
Look at small doable pieces.
And reach the daily goals you set.

Take care of each day.
Finish it with a satisfying sigh.
Each day, live up to the best side of you.
And let any negative energy pass you by.

The stars will tell your story.
They will come to life and shine full bright.
Crickets will chirp and birds will sing,
For you…

Everything will be alright.

Kayla Elfers

Centereach Students, NY 11755

Numbed niceties near negligent nobodies
On sidewalks smoking cigarettes. Centereach Students:
Perms, proms, and plightful problems of
Who gets the shit kicked out of them
Behind bleachers barricading bums from
Students so (not) sharp. With their
Walkmans they walk home and change
To travel to teen's territory:
House party at
Kathy's with kegs.
Shannon shotguns a beer
While Lynda lets loose
While Bobby barfs in the bathroom
While Neal knocks out a nerd.
An unforgettable night with unforgettable people.
Next day no one knows
Neal Got suspended.
Bobby barfed on the bus ride to Centereach.
Lynda passed her test! It's positive.
Shannon's shades only hid her hangover for three periods.
But someday soon everyone will know
What happened in Centereach.
Numbed niceties near negligent nobodies.
Invisible individuals, ireful internally in the moment
But these negligent nobodies
In twenty years or so
Will become somethings much more

On a little Island once infatuated with interpersonal memories
But now isolated in intrapersonal growth.
Just like these teens,
Centereach changed
And grew to become a better
School for its students.

Melissa E. Filippelli

Unsung

She was a hero in her own right
A steadfast, a constant
An understated, ever-present force---
On standby
Ready to act
Ever so necessary
Yet never fully seen or appreciated
She was unsung…
As lethal as she was healing
As fierce as she was gentle
As determined as she was generous
What a soul!
Capable and understanding
Available in times of need
Her meekness concealing her courage
Her quiet nature masking her bold soul
On standby
Ready to act
Ever so necessary.

Adam D Fisher

Identity

I'm at a cocktail party
walking around the room.
I ask a man in a gray suit,
maroon tie, " Are you Adam Fisher?"
"No. Sorry I don't know him."
I turn to a man in a blue sweater,
blond hair, "Are you Adam Fisher?"
"No. Who is that?"
 I asked a bald man in a tweed jacket,
"Are you Adam Fisher?"
"No. Never heard
of him."
I go to all the men
in the room with
the same question.
One man responds,
"No. Aren't you Adam Fisher?"
That's how I found out
who I was.

Ginamarie Foceri

She lost herself some years back
Too many of them now to keep track
The time was marked on her body
Her scars, proudly displayed like a painting in a lobby.

For these marked the love that once lived within her
With a pot of emotions, almost too heavy to stir
They tried defining the woman she will be
For those scars were all the world wanted to see

No cries for help ever left her lips
For she knew power lived in her finger tips.
Pride and fearlessness, she wore like a badge of honor
She never knew the brink of greatness was upon her

To heal, that was all that was left
Overthinking and self-sabotage, these habits she must neglect.
And self-love she must perfect.

To better oneself, Is a lifelong journey
Focused and determined to relearn me

Excuse me while I put on my crown
Lioness, Or Queen to you, never forget I am more than worthy.
What you thinks will never concern

Rich Follett

nine eleven

the towers fell;
we
did not.

America
still sings:
chords of
courage,
strains of
hope
ring true.

years later,
i marvel at
leaves of grass
springing from
the fecund rubble of
dreams
that did not die.

America
still sings -
(lilac will
sweetly scent
dooryards
many millennia
hence).

the towers fell;
we
did not.

John M Fraioli

Peel Away

Peel back the sun
infinite night
awaits

Sleep now
as you never could before
Old soul
homeward bound

There is always
another journey to take

The body will
nurture the Earth
and those who come next

Peel back your mask
no more hiding
Naked and beautiful
a new light
across the ever expanding night

Peace is yours at last

William Frank

The Royal Easter Festival at Tulip Cottage

It was a sunny April day at Tulip Cottage
  for the Easter event hosted by the Queen,
  at the back of the estate on Paschal Green,
Certainly not the place to find glissades of carnage.

Pony rides, hay carts, races, a carousel,
  a splendid festival for village and family
  until the Egg hunt when, in spasms of ecstasy,
scores of children tangled in trees or dropped in a well.

Today, the Palace released a statement
  after most children were recovered and sent home
but four others, in a case of gross mismanagement
  by the Royal Expedition Office were sent
to the Arctic where an orca washed them off an ice floe
  and they were eaten. The Palace regrets the incident.

Bob Freville

Offal

I wade in the muck of Venetian Shores
As the murky water chokes me,
Shimmering in its predictability
As the parking lot swells with beach goers.
A brilliant ennui envelopes me
As the water wrinkles my flesh
And the tiki bar is choked by drunks
with farmer's tans and collapsible chairs.
There is no life raft,
Just as there is no point.
The sun burns my eyes
As the Pepto pink alcohol runs down the block of ice,
Finding its home in the fetid bellies of mouth-breathing Lawn Guylinders.
Swindlehurst is our Venice
But its Renaissance is a gluttony.
And the sun says it's spoiled
As the seagulls all gather.

Nicole Fuschetti

Daughter of Water

Rolling across the backs
        of seals
     she lays her foamy sea spray
          onto the fuzzy feathers of penguins,
In the north- she is bitter and cold,
        frozen in glaciers of ice
          with only the heat of the polar bear's step
     to warm her chilled soul,
south is where she runs free
        merrily swirling around bubble-tip anemone
          as whispers of pterios and eel wander
            through the churning expanse,
          still--
the furthest depths are quiet blackness,
        her refuge
          her prison,
     the glowing monsters that pop and crack like firecrackers
     appear and all too quickly fade
          hidden in the abyss is life
            she has never even seen
        yet the sun captivates her
            as much as the night
and ascending like a tsunami
        she crashes upon the sandy shore
          letting beads and bubbles evaporate
   into the clouds
        until they are silvered saturated nebulas

that volley back into the earth
        giving life to the rising sea of trees
                as the fire-filled sun dances upon them.

M. Frances Garcia

The Avon Lady
In Memory of Mom

She arrived every other week
wearing a smile and
a pleated blue skirt with pebbled
tan tote bag in tow. Inside,
there was the latest Avon book:
Mom and I could not
wait to have a look, peruse the pages,
select a new cologne, get some Skin So Soft (SSS) bath oil
which repelled bugs too; or, for me, a light blue lipstick for
teens that turned different
colors according to the
warmth of your lips, the
feel of your mood on any given
summer afternoon.
We used to
spend time on the beach
circling
the items we wanted
in red pen,
and Mom even began
a collection of Avon fashion
watches to match her
bright outfits for family gatherings, weddings
and anniversary celebrations over the years.
Then, there were funerals too, with salty tears.
Those watch straps were navy or black.

Of course, we always had
to pare down the initial list
of what we wanted from
the Avon brochure
to just the most
essential items because
(let's face it) not everything
was on sale and bills had
just come again in the mail.
When The Avon Lady left, there
was always more laundry to do
for seven young children,
(most days you did at least three)
and dinner still had to
be made; perhaps
you threw together
some caponata with fresh eggplant,
which was your favorite Italian dish.

When I think of you, Mom,
I remember happiness
before the years went by
and times became harder,
when Dad passed away
of congestive heart failure
nine years ago;
then uncle, Fr. Jim, also left us at 92.
Who ever could have known such
a sorrowful view?
At some point, even The Avon Lady was gone.
Yet in her memory, I began
to sell Avon, too (mostly for the discount)

and once I even earned
an intricate, cream colored porcelain doll, with gold trim,
The Albee Award, for selling ten grand. It was,
you would say, an accomplishment, though
that prize is no longer offered these days.

Everything is done online now,
including the brochures
with pages that flip at
the touch of a button
on my computer screen. The personal visit
is replaced with technology.
And you are gone now, Mom,
for well over two years already. How can that be true?
What am I now, without you? I know that
you would tell me that you had to go to God.
Your journey here was complete.
I know that you lived each day as gift
to your family. I miss and still remember you, Mom,
your warm smile as we greeted The Avon Lady down
on Hamilton Ave. in Oyster Bay
every other week. Sometimes, we would share coffee with her in the kitchen;
and
our laughter carried through the air as we
browsed the Avon book and made our final selections.

Life became a series of rocky mountains we had to climb; even with
rope and nylon webbing, our anchor extensions were
sometimes too short to summit.
Time was not our friend. And yet, in the end, for a few
minutes, we were able to forget life's harsh
weather conditions. We remained brave in the eye

of a hurricane.

How could I ever ask for more
than what your friendship was to me,
as we set up our pop up tents
along the shore each day?
I kept all the camp gear, your floral bathing suit, sandy beach shoes,
weathered pumice stones, and your collection of Avon costume jewelry
watches,
even the ones that stopped keeping time.
They are mine to recall every bit of all that we shared, without apology
but with immense gratitude and appreciation.
You are in another, better place now, they all say.
You grace Eternity with your kind presence, dear Mom,
and your Spirit echoes inside the catalog of my heart.

Now, and forevermore,
I hold onto the simple joy
of The Avon Lady
knocking on our front door.

Tina Lechner Gibbons

Apologies To My Parents

Mom

You were the one—
the first to stir my imagination
reading me stories of
royal elephants in far off lands
and then showing me it
was possible to create my own tales
of fantasy journeys to imaginary places.
Where I could be whatever
I wanted to be.
You were the strong one -
the one I wanted to be like -
the one who tried to
guide me
support me.
I'm sorry -
I'm sorry about the wooden headboard.
The one I took the nail file to
and deeply etched the horrid words
I hate you.
I don't remember why
but I still feel the coarse
steel file between
my fingers
as I slowly
m e t h o d i c a l l y -
angrily carved

I
HATE
YOU
You saw it—
It made you cry
You rarely cried—unless it was death
and I made you cry.
The headboard avenged you
So many times I would awake
from a bad dream
& hit my head on it
I cursed that headboard over and over.
I'm sorry I made you cry.
I'm sorry I didn't say
           I love you more often.

Dad

I wasn't the daughter
You wanted me to be
But then I'm really not sure
What you wanted.
Just a little girl in ribbons & bows
& pink frilly dresses.
That little girl dressed in her mother's
Cut down cocktail dresses – dressed as Anna
from the King and I, as she watched the TV
Westerns with you, toy gun slung at her side
Annie Oakley hat on her head,
wooden horse between her legs.
Little girl who played tea party with Patty Playpal and
Tiny Tears, with her Zorro cape draped around her neck, and
mask hid her identity.
Little girl that stared at the little boys from

Her Bronx apartment window – apartment 3C –
Watching as they played in the courtyard –
C'mon dad – you should have known I was going to be
A hopeless romantic – The name of our street was
Valentine. What did you expect?
The little girl who, left behind the ribbons and lace
For bellbottoms, halter tops, cigarettes, and boys
(mmmm maybe I kept that Zorro whip)
You didn't know who I was becoming – you
Just saw the little girl – that you tried to cloister…
I didn't know who I was becoming
All I knew was I wasn't the perfect good girl
I wasn't anybody else but me, no matter how
Much you wanted me to be ….
But then… you weren't who I wanted you to be
The perfect TV dad – even the dad I saw others had…
I didn't know your story – the battle scars
The nightmares, the PTSD –
What I saw, was you
Angry, bitter, sitting in your pleather black recliner
Cigar in one hand
Scotch in the other
Your silent stories – bottled up inside
Both of us prisoners to your past
I came to understand too late
I'm sorry.
(don't forget the dolls closet –
I hope it's waiting for me on the other side)

Anthony Gentile

Those Nights

When I smell the ocean, I see your face
Sun soaked tresses dripping with amber hues
Sweet, sultry lips smiling, sensual and soft
Eyes deep as the ocean, misty, mysterious

When I smell the ocean, I see your ghost
Haunted by longing, a scent, a smile
A wave broken on the sea shore
Precious memories scattered about like foam

I remember those nights
Bellowing breeze, bourbon induced babbling
You, me, flickering fire
And promises of eternity

My heart breaks now
Surreptitiously slipping away from solace
Pensively penning its poems
Loving you through tear stained pages

Martha Gimenez

At Pinelawn

Some pray reverently,
in disbelief

Some set up lawn chairs,
to keep company
in infinite loneliness

Some trim the grass
and brush off weeds
and wipe away stains
and oil the plaque
and arrange the flowers
and try to make up
for not having done more before

They all nod at one another
in the distance
or in the walkway
and force themselves to think,

"He liked the birch trees here. They are always so beautiful."

Selena Goetschius

Left With My Heart

One year without you
I had to face my fears
You've been gone for too long
I can't breath through all these tears

I still ask 'why?'
But it's a question I already know
It was past due time
You were well prepared to go

I still hear my screams echo
The ones from when I first cried
I begged and begged and begged
I Just wanted some more time

'One more day' I pleaded
But I would say it the next day too
No time would ever be enough
I guess 19 years must make do

The oceans that I sob
The screams I have let out
I say it feels so empty
But I feel it every time I shout

It's not an empty feeling
It's full of grief and pain

I Cried every single day
It took forever to maintain

Even to this day
The tears fall every week
I beg for you to visit
Even if you just leave a kiss on my cheek

One year without you
Yet I still hear the flat line
When your heart stopped
You took and left with mine

Gloria Gordon

She Roars

There are days
when she forgets
to worry
but only about herself

Her plate is never empty
as she takes on
the problems of the world

She's tackled
the C word
and danced over it

For her own mother
she has
slammed the door
when the grim reaper
came to call
she shouted at Satan
not today devil
not today
yet when she attends
a friend's funeral
the tears flow down her cheeks

She tip toes softly
 but roars loudly

84

Her mate
never suffers alone
she shares his miseries
and joys of life

She is a Leo
queen of the jungle
she roars

Paul Thomas Grecco

Our blanket

Hot
Unfolded
It coughs
like some pyschic
Bedouin imprints.
A bright dust forms
where the red sea hills
throttle the night.
It's whole the mess
that comes with being us
It's French grave dirt.
A half-cupped
pronounciation of Atlas,
the desert end of love,
of life,
with the irony of flowers
ever-presently marked.

Aaron Griffin

How To Change Some Body

This is you how change some body,
in an extra special way,
that redefines their outlook,
and adds magic to their day.

Find someone out there,
anywhere,
that's bored of how they are,
someone who yearns for something new,
Now here's the way to start:

We'll take this business man,
dressed to impress,
but all alone,
in an elevator car, playing on his mobile phone.

What game?

"Snake", huh?

He's skilled, the highest score I've ever seen.
But why should snaking skills like that be wasted on a screen?

We'll ride the wind of change with him,
and set his ship asail,
let's leave his top alone for now,
and give this man

a tail.

We just whisper to him nicely,
because persuasion never fails,
we start his change off softly,
and murmur to him:

"Tail",

a perfect snakey word to slither down his hearing tubes,
and nestle deep into his brain like titillating news,

"tail",

a word so warm and thrilling,
to coil deep into his mind,

"tail",

something he didn't ask for,
that we know he's gonna like,

"tail",

interrupting people business,
slinking,
slinking,
down his spine,

"tail",

demanding his attention,

"tail",

a word on the attack,
making its magic happen,
and sprouting from his back.

Now we've put the gears in motion,
the summoned limb emerges fast,
restrained only by the stitching of his polyester pants.

With trousers tearing at the rear,
the failing fabric holds no more,
several kilograms of python

THUMP

upon the checkered floor.

Already a full meter long, unrolling itself out,
he knows at once,
that tail,
is HIS!

He's rather weirded out.

He's not sure
if it's just a dream,
but despite his lasting doubt,
he feels the muscles,
flex,
as the appendage writhes about.

He feels cold tile beneath his scales,

forgets what he is doing,
as his senses tell him tales
of only being partly human.

And there he goes,
tugging at his rear
with both his hands,
attempting to remove the thing,
from where it stays attached.

But there's more snake trapped inside him,
spouting outwards from his spine,
and in his grasp it slithers out,
with iridescent scaly shine.

His heart is pounding in his chest,
tail draped across his shoes,
yet the part of him
that's troubled
by the changes
starts to lose.

He knows there's something pleasant here,
something he
might
learn to love,

So let's help him with suggestions
for some changes up above.

We'll speak a little louder,
so we won't have to repeat,
increased volume,

brings quicker results,
so we make sure he can hear,
unseen, we utter to him:

"Face,"

and vanish off his ears.

His sinuses are twitching,
like he'd breathed a pepper twister,
with a metamorphic sneeze,
he honks away his human sniffer,
a reptile snout erupts from where his nose had been before,
through slit pupils he sees himself
reflected in the door,

Agape, his mouth reveals
two fangs
fit for a carnivore,
and fingers frisk his scaly scalp,
for hair that is no more.

Watch him panic-dialing on his phone,
to call for an assist,
but when the operator's on the line,
all he can say is,

"Hissssss."

Goodness, did you hear that hiss?
He really meant it too!

He can use snake language fluently,
as though he always knew.

Still attempting to preserve himself,
grasping his snout with hope,
he tries to
collapse
his muzzle down,
like it's a telescope.

His two-pronged tongue
extends,
flicking out to taste the air,
catching tired office scents that
permeate the corporate lair,
and a certain smell that rings a bell,
so distinct and so peculiar,
the human smell of people parts we hadn't banished sooner.

Those arms,
those legs,
that torso,
dressed for sorting business mail,
now finding themselves sandwiched,
between a serpent head and tail.

He goes through the act of panicking
because he guesses that he should -
But he knows inside,
he'd love to keep on changing if he could.

Like most people,
he's liking this more than he'd dare expect.

To help him out,
and keep him going,
we whisper gently to him:

"Neck",

after far to many hours bent unmoving at his desk,
unshackled from the strain,

"neck",

releases all the stress,
relaxes,
lengthens,
lengthens,

"neck",

stretching on and on,
giving scales to
every
added
centimeter
as it
spawns,

"neck",

morphing into a serpent's
in a fluid forward motion,
a sensation rush to rival an intoxicating potion,

making the thought
of staying person-shaped
a most regretful notion.

He feels it's right,
accepts it now,
he WANTS to be a snake.

So we'll finish up our task,
it would be cruel to make him wait.

We say:

"Let go of those two heavy
hands,
kick away those aching
feet,
dump that human
chest and belly,
and your change will be complete."

With a pile of empty clothing there,
placed to catch his fall,
he sticks the landing,
python-formed,
coils, scales, and all.

He embraces what has happened,
if not entirely believing,
and finds his unplanned serpentdom
relaxing and relieving.

He cooperated with us well,

94

so we owe him our respect,
We'll provide an explanation,
so that our target isn't vexed:

"Yep, that handsome beast is you,
and this is absolutely real!

You get to be a creature!

Isn't that an awesome deal?

You morphed with all the flare your human language could evoke,
a transformation subject better suited than I hoped!"

Waiting not a moment more,
he gives slithering a try,
and he masters legless movement
before he gives a reply -

in which he gaily hisses to us,
with a drowsy, snaky, sigh.

After a thrilling change like that,
I say a nap here suits him fine.

Since it's late,
he can enjoy the lift,
alone,
for quite some time.

Now he's coiled atop those vacant garments,
comfy and content,
no longer stressed by people thoughts like

how he'll pay the rent.

So this is where we'll leave him.
I'm sure he'll be okay from here.

If animal control is called,
he has nothing to fear.

For a critter seeking pampering,
the zoo has high appeal,
free meals that Paul from auditing
will never get to steal,
and climbing trees,
and swimming ponds,
and hollowed logs for hiding under,
tall jungle grass to slither through,
a warm lamp to aid in slumber.

If he stays like this,
or changes back,
that choice is up to him -

his human form's still hidden,
just beneath that serpent skin.

But as for us, we're done here.

Friend, my lesson is complete -

You know how to change
some body.

So I
now,
shall take my leave.

Valerie Griggs

The Haves

When I see the 3500 square foot house,
I imagine someone who treasured their
God-given aptitudes and turned them
into purpose and delight, who achieved
something. And this person found a partner,
a pal, a co-conspirator to complement,
collaborate; someone who got it the same
way, shared the vision, the joke, the passion
for the punch, the playfulness; to push it,
pass it, kick it off, or kick back, kick up a storm.
A dynamic duo who loved living it, giving it,
digging it together all along, all the way
and then they created other people –
new lives, minds hearts imaginations for the
world, the times. When I see that impossibly
huge house, my heart skips – how much love, risk,
sweat celebration holds up that house? I feel like
the home team is winning, there are human beings
being human making, building, sharing, turning
skill into generations at one table, family
love, loyalty, contentment, all that matters when
nothing is left. Everything the bastards hate: a name,
a clan, a heritage of everyday people, not kings
or despots, not thugs, oligarchs or lucifers. That big
house belongs to hands doing an honest day's work
better than most because of how much they love
each other, and that house says, we are alive here.

George Guida

Back on Easy Street

I never said a man was not
the sum of his parts.
The labor is what matters,
how you fasten parts together
for the ride through local streets,
down distant highways,
into dead ends.

The hardest part of tightening
a connection comes
when you realize
you don't have the tools
and try anyway,
a decision.

I am not an insightful man.
If I were, I would have said
"person."
I would have left the cars off
the street, invisible here
but easy to find
as the need to know
you can keep traveling
and forget how that happens.

Maureen Hadzick- Spisak

The Originator

Before there was time
The Great Imagination
　stared at the vast emptiness
　and decided to create a playground.
It would be no larger than a grain of sand
　in the sandbox of the universe.
The Great Imagination stood back
　and tossed out a flaming ball of fire.
Into it He placed the sun and the moon
　which see-sawed back and forth
　creating splinters of day and night.
He clapped his hands and mountains
　formed and only he could move them.
He was so happy with his creation
　His laughter filled the sky
　slid down the mountains and into the sea.
Crimson, fuchsia and turquoise
　flashed before his eyes
He sprinkled smooth, rough, and feathery seeds
　that became the trees and bushes
　with leaves that would swing in glorious greetings.
He added sweet smelling honeysuckle
　to please the birds and butterflies
　that were yet to come.

The Great Imagination delighted in His creation
   picturing the joy it would bring
   to the daughters and grand daughters
   of the Goddess Gaia.

Geneva Hagar

Flip the Coin

Must I enter hell to fly through heaven?
Must I leave my dignity at the gate, remove
my shoes and belt, toss my needed toiletries
and watch the pat-down of wheelchair disabled?
Fear of fear is taking hours away from normal
and cannot be returned. Set me free to make
my choice in taking chances.
A bird flies amongst danger.

Nick Hale

Just Boys

The test scores came back.
They're just boys.
They'll catch up.

      Okay then.

Reading was a challenge
and answers, expensive.
They're just boys

      what do you expect?

Dropped off in a squad car
from a fight over who's tougher
charged as adults at 15
but they're just boys
and will be boys

      right?

They're **just boys**
what can you expect?
      Nothing
with that attitude.

In an alternate timeline, I expect
the specialists

the tutors
the supplemental jump-start
the diligent support
and the challenge to rise to
will engage low-genius IQ, under-achieving potential felons.

I expect diplomas and speeches, honors and degrees.
I expect science fair medals, wrestling trophies, and standing ovations.
I expect a future
and prepare them for a future
to take my place,
keep it warm
for the next "just" boys.

J. Peter Hansen

High Above the Water

Drowning in our fears, no hope in sight
We hear the sirens all through the night
Hold down the fort and continue to fight
Turn all this darkness, into the light

> We better hold our heads
> High above the water
> Hold on tight
> When we're sinking low

> We better hold our heads
> High above the water
> Hold on tight
> In the end we'll know

We prayed to the Lord, got down on our knees
Send in the troops, maybe the Calvary
This ain't the way it's supposed to be
And then came an answer, he helped us to see

> We better hold our heads
> High above the water
> Hold on tight
> When we're sinking low

> We better hold our heads
> High above the water

Hold on tight
In the end we'll know

Hold up the colors, they are yellow and blue
We hope for miracles to help us through
So send us a sign, tell us what to do
We are the victims but our hearts still ring true

    We better hold our heads
    High above the water
    Hold on tight
    When we're sinking low

    We better hold our heads
    High above the water
    Hold on tight
    In the end we'll know

Robert L. Harrison

The Bus Route

The bus is packed
with green card holders,
dropping off nannies
and day laborers,
while picking up house maids
and wanderers alike.
As the traffic slows
the bus to a crawl
thoughts of being late
spread back to
the rear seats.
Finally, the last
stop is reached
and the tide
of people leave
in search of new
beginnings.
The new Americans
fan out fast.

Damian Ward Hey

In Your Stooping Age
(To my father)

When I was quite young,
you were a dolphin
I clung to through the depths
of a swimming pool.

As I grew older,
you became a horse,
and I rode on your back
through the yard's badlands.

A little later,
we were pioneers
tramping those first footpaths
through the cumbrous woods.

And once I was grown
you were just yourself
in one equal measure
mirrored through my blood.

Now, as I am gray,
you abide with me
in your stooping, white age
of softened angles,

that when I turn grave,

you'll be there, much more
than dolphin, or than horse,
or even pioneer.

William Heyen

Nesconset Orioles

Early evening the oriole's song just before she quiets into her tear-
      shaped nest

in the pear tree in the village of our childhood outside our bedroom when
      my brother was alive

as her notes then when my older brother Werner was alive
      as her notes then.

Sheila Hoffenberg

My Thoughts Are Your Interest

I love to write, I love to read
Pen and paper is all I need
To share one thought or two or three
Of interest to you, a gift from me

To be absorbed in a catching way
That brings such joy with what I say
Knowledge will bring you up to date
Will turn your mind in a different state

A topic I'll pick to make you wonder
As you read through the night with rain and thunder
Or at the beach while on the sand
A smile for sure, my book in demand

To be published with patience and time
I'll be ready whenever on the drop of a dime
It's never too late for a writing career
Will keep at it, for there's nothing I fear

My thoughts will appear in a story or poem
Whether I am out or typing at home
Research of meanings before I begin
Will bring truth and maybe just a touch of fiction

My imagination will deepen to make it come alive
I'll put all I know to keep it in strive
A memoir, an essay or even a prose
Never know what it'll be, it's a feat I chose

Whatever the outcome of writing a book
I'll be grateful and happy no matter how long it took
Achievement and honor for which I am in control
Of being called an author, my future, my role

Arnold Hollander

Ukraine

The other day
We had a home
From which our lives circulate.

The other day
We went to school
And mingled with our classmates.

The other day
We visited our library
To satisfy what our homework dictates.

Today
Shelling destroyed
Our home, our school, and our library.

Today
We, those still alive,
Hide in basements from Russian flunkies.

Today
We have to leave
Our homes and families

Today
We have another
Holocaust

Kevin Holmes

Faith simple

How many words for God
How many Gods for words
Like overspray splits here there
And I'm our pockets
A history of faces in intervals
Ming vases cave paintings
Walks and halls full of God
Walls and stalls
Oh God we go on and on
Putting
You in cages of books
Pages of films movies shorts longs
Wall paper signed an unsigned
Revolutions just wars
 Crusades to rule
Oh God I miss you
There was no time
Alone
No telephone
Besides you where
I couldn't find but you're never gone
Besides
-I believe

Larry Jaffe

The Final Prison

This is the final prison
it is the end of an eternal sentence
of incarcerating spirit in physical universe
of spirit groveling to matter

> – Thus, we end all games
> – Thus, we end all entreaties
> – Thus, we end all sacrifices

This is the final prison
it is the end of the enforcement
of spirit converged with body
of body overwhelmed with serpent

> – Thus, we end all pain
> – Thus, we end all tyranny
> – Thus, we end all oppression

This is the final prison
it is the era of spirit invulnerable
of spirit unbending
of spirit not breaking

> – Thus, the spirit has been set free
> – Thus, the spirit has been set free
> – Thus, the spirit is free

Gloria Jainchill

I'm Getting Older

The song Landslide comes to mind with the lyrics I'm getting older,
The music and melody dances, plays inside of me,
It lifts my spirts, now hanging low, as summer's last breezes blow.

I think upon summer days of old, chasing lightning bugs and flying kites,
With siblings and friends on Long Island August nights,
A bonfire to warm cool arms, parents chatting by the fire's light.

The dating in our days of youth, was holding hands and sneaking a kiss,
Walking along sidewalks on De Wolf, Prospect, Sixth and Fifth.
Looking up at the stars, planning futures with no thoughts of Mars.

In 1969 we landed a man on the moon, my parents amazed and awed.
Born before cars were our main source of transportation,
City carts were pulled by horses to deliver milk, breads, ice and sausages.

Woodstock Music Festival that same year, with its laughter and its tears,
Opened the doors of heart and spirit for others not as privileged.
We began to change the world and quality of life for others.

Desegregation was born a new, we lost Bobby and Martin Luther King, too.
We listened to Bob Hope, Lawrence Welk, watched black and white television,
The Rifleman, Howdy Doodie, Red Skelton, Roy Rogers and Dale Evans.

The Beatles broke standards of protocols with their long hair and lyrics,
We listened to long playing records, 45's and cassettes,

Fleetwood Mac, Barry McGuire, Johnny Mathis, Dean Martin and Andy Williams.

Now facing another crisis in life and passing time, I ask myself,
Do I stay in my home, now too big, or rent a place for $2,000 a month?
I gasp in shock, the thought of spending that much for a 2-bedroom apartment!

When I retired in a state of bliss the money was enough to exist.
Retired ten years now, I struggle over where I can afford to live.
Downsizing, a smaller footprint, is good but can I do this?

In short, getting older is a bitch,
But, I have loved each year and every inch.

Alma Johnson

Reluctant appreciation

In the stillness of the morning, I rise
Sluggishly greeting this day that ends the miserable, chaotic challenges of
the WEEK.
The sound of the angry Howling wind speaks the opposite of my tired
appreciation of the reminder of my breath loaned by a faithful creator.

Alyssa Johnson

Winter Victims

Looking through my lonely Bedroom window, I see other LONELY victims. The pale grass waiting to welcome the SPRING. I see an Isolated Blue shed jailed by Mr. Winter. There on the ground are two lost soccer balls waiting to be found by the careless children that left them there last summer.

Ryan Jones

To Shivers In The End

We fail to remember
Our mistakes from the past
Their lessons left behind
In pursuit of our hopes
Charging through our limitations
Only to be ensnared by them
Same old problem
Strange new context

Did we truly forget
Or was hope too tempting
The mind over matter
Fate over Remembrance
The lessons of past wrongs are harsh
Do we run, cower, or fight them
Setting the trap
To catch ourselves

Sight pinned fast on hope's light
One can miss the pitfalls
And who can see them all
When rushing to our hopes
Yet without a thought for the past
Calamity can strike again
Mistakes, useless
Regrets, worthless

The tunnel envelops
Traversed without hindsight
Strengthened by our attempts
Aired out by force of will
The blind fool is no worse off here
Than the cautious, circumspect fool
The captive light
Reveals nothing

Our errors, like vengeance
Come, go, and then return
We can never unlearn
What nature has ingrained
Each of us, driven by forces
That brought us to our advancement
Tools that helped us
Now betray us

Lured by increasing gains
We surge forth with designs
Must we lose to improve
Loss until all is lost
Ignorant of reality
We seek out the whims of our fates
Endless follies
Until fatal

Our dreams are now shattered
Our wills are now shattered
Our minds are now shattered
Our souls are now shattered

We have thought and acted in vain
To shivers our hearts have shattered
Useless pieces
Left where they lie

Sara Jones

Glazing Over

Talking, talking, talking endlessly
About the price of things,
When the most valuable things are free.
The sun shines through the window
On a bright winter day.
Listen, I see your mouth moving
But I hear birds singing sweetly
and your words are a discordant hum.
You're speaking words tumbling
Through French horn shaped pipe dreams.
I'm smiling, thinking of being
Everywhere else.

Edward Kenny

Calverton

He spent years in New Guinea,
Served in almost every state,
He left this life too early,
I'm visiting him too late.

Malaria and Jungle Rot,
And the air raids took their toll,
A soldier gives all he's got,
He gave his body and soul.

And they've been waiting for the moment,
When they'll visit with their son,
All through the time of their interment,
Waiting here at Calverton.
And they've been waiting great and silent,
Just like their generation,
Although their times were lean and violent,
They're at peace in Calverton.

She was the love of his life,
And he was her dream come true,
A loyal and faithful wife,
And a husband always true.

He preceded her so long,
It was over thirty years,
Through that time she was so strong,
Not permitting public tears.

And they've been waiting for the moment,
When they'll visit with their son,
All through the time of their interment,
Waiting here at Calverton.
And they've been waiting great and silent,
Just like their generation,
Although their times were lean and violent,
They're at peace in Calverton.

For her a bunch of flowers,
And for him the Stars and Stripes,
After we talked for hours,
Came the distant sound of pipes.

And they've been waiting for the moment,
When they'll visit with their son,
All through the time of their interment,
Waiting here at Calverton.
And they've been waiting great and silent,
Just like their generation,
Although their times were lean and violent,
They're at peace in Calverton.

Daniel Kerr

The Breadth of God

As we stood together before the Wailing Wall in Jerusalem,
my Israeli host and friend Ilan proudly said,
"It all started here."

I kept hearing Ilan's words as I visited Masada,
Nazareth,
The Synagogue at Capernaum,
The Sea of Galilee,
The Garden of Gethsensamie,
The Via Delarosa,
and the Church of the Holy Sceplacular.

Perhaps I heard Ilan's words most clearly,
as I stood before the Dome of the Rock.

Here is where:
Abraham was to sacrifice Isaac,
Solomon and Herod built their temples,
and the Prophet Mohammed ascended Buraq,
the traditional heavenly steed of the prophets,
for his passage to heaven.

Father Abraham would no doubt be pleased,
that the tree branches of his family,
Jews, Christians, and Muslims,
revere this spot so many years later.

Admiring the simple beauty of the Dome of the Rock,
I remembered a time I entered a mosque in Cape Town.
As I quietly took off my shoes,
an imam seated on the floor beckoned me in.
It was a mystical place,
and I felt the breadth of God on my neck,
as I often do in churches, synagogues, and temples around the world.

At the funeral of murdered journalist Daniel Pearl,
an Iman spoke of the shared values of the three Abrahamic faiths.

"If to be a Jew means to say with all one's heart, mind and soul,
"hear O Israel, the Lord our God, the Lord is One,
not only today I am a Jew,
I have always been one."

"If to be a Christian means to love the Lord God our Lord with all my heart,
mind and soul, and to love for my fellow human being what I love for myself,
then I am not only a Christian,
but I have always been one."

"And I am here to inform you,
with the full authority of the Quaranic texts and the practices of the Prophet
Mohammad,
to say May Allah's Peace, Mercy and Blessings be upon all of you,
is no different."

If the three quarrelling children of Abraham,
could find the courage to focus on their shared values,
perhaps the breadth of the God they worship,
would help cool this overheated world.

Mindy Kronenberg

Jelly Bean Breakfast

When you were six you got up early
one morning to make yourself a
jelly bean breakfast—
a bright bowl of colorful stones
shining in a circle of milk.

I was lurching toward the table
in my adult fog, considering the cereals
that beckoned reason: practical grain pellets,
stodgy pillows of shredded wheat,
brown flakes wilting under the weight of minerals.

Your face beamed, tiny teeth glittering
in a proud grin. You lifted a spoonful
of rainbow like a proud chef,
and in a flash I dreamed of the world
you would one day be in,

where lullabies faded into
stern admonitions, the joyful
improvised dance giving way
to a tight smile over folded arms.
And I joined you in your culinary escapade.

Joan Kuchner

Lacrosse Mom

hands clasped and unclasped
locked and unlocked
elbows barely supported her body
as she swayed forward
eyes tracking her son on the field

a stranger to me
as I sat at the other end of the bench
next to my son and grandson
yet waves of her emotions
reached me
broke over me
threw me into another time

my son on the same field
my wanting the ball in his stick
wanting him to shine
fearing there would be an error
the season was ending
the team needed to succeed
he needed to succeed
this game made a difference

clenched and unclenched
my fingernails left a line of bloody dots on my palms
across the generations I could feel the pain
embedded in the dream

Tara Lamberti

Pepper

Our relationship began as more of an angst at first bite situation.
You put holes in my brand new school clothes with your tiny needle teeth.
I sat on the kitchen floor crying, covered in scrapes, scratches, and puncture marks.
Why didn't you just want to cuddle me?
You looked like a Chuck Jones cartoon: a puff of black smoke with a set of chompers. Maybe I was an annoying kid. Always trying to pet you and hold you. Maybe you were a bratty baby too. Maybe we were too much alike in some ways. Nobody could make you do something you didn't want to do. You were a primal creature. On many nights when something inside you sparked, you climbed on top of one of the junkers in the back yard - not

the hood but the *roof* of the car -black flames waving behind you in the wind as you holwed at the Moon. I see you standing there in my minds eye, this mystic Earth-bound being, praying to your true Master. One look in those older, soulful, honey brown eyes and I knew I would take a pilgrimage just to meet you atop a mountain. You were to be revered. You became my Familiar. My first true love. And when you left this plane, a bit of my magic went with you.

Billy Lamont

when i write

my friends are poets, writers,
philosophers, thinkers, prophets,
musicians and artists,
from throughout the ages,
that i read about in books

dear reader
perhaps in some simple way
i could be that for you

words spoken from my intimate core
i can"t surppress this passion and inspiration anymore

to be or not to be-
the art within the art within the art within the art within the art
I want to feel- to have heart
to be real- to one day be the art!

brave enough to break down the healthy
or unhealthy boundary
that separates you from me
leaving only vulnerability
tearing down the fourth wall!
left only with the hope,
to one day, finally find
intimacy

i've broken the glass bubble of identity
reaching for your hand with sincerity
spiritual love is all inclusive
spiritual love knows no boundary
rather than alienation- i will always choose community!
stay connected/stay connected/stay connected
to be the change in the world
you and i want to see
i choose to live with integrity
to be the LOVE, be the LOVE, be the LOVE
to be the PEACE, to be the PEACE, to be the PEACE
i choose community over alienation!

soul metamorphosis
crucifixion
and resurrection
a poet that is a poem
a creation that can create
may your very soul be a great poem!
our life is a message!
a string of pearls

society keeps telling me,
"you cannot write today.
you have too many responsibilities"-
but when i do write
i will be ferrocious!
when i write
the page will bleed with light!
when i write
when i write!

Linda Leff

Perseverance Pears

Fire-charged winds whip tirelessly,
attacking stocky hidden branches, flames rising,
savagely smoking the growing cycle scaring
tender pear skins of the delicate fruit.

Untamable fire sweeping non-stop up the heated hillside.
Terminating the life-blood of newly arrived migrant pickers.
Pickers that could not change the date, nor the sad fate,
of an anticipated harvest of previously perfect pears.

Standing alongside delipidated trucks, loaded with family
members and limited supplies, wood ladders roped tightly
to the old truck, human bodies feel the intolerable heat,
staring into erupting flames, watching their needed wages burn.

Waterless wildfires that erased the colors of the hills.
Only black remains on formerly thriving portions of earth.
Juicy and sweet pale green pears, now beaten fruit,
scorched and viciously struck down, traumatized
and conquered, by nature's wicked sweep.

Nya née Masonya Legerme

Opt Out

I am here to return my adulting pass.
Yep, I'm done.
No more bills to pay.
I am officially on the run.

Who needs money?
I'm strictly here for the fun.
Running wild in the park.
Roasting marshmallows in the sun.

Maybe I'll host sidewalk shows.
Teach my kitten and pup how to do tricks.
Get some school kids to tip them.
Gather all the coins so we can buy chicken kebab sticks.

I think I'll just live in my car.
Go on a never ending journey.
Keep on running until I can't anymore.
Until I get a message from the most High that helps me gain more.

I'm seriously going to opt out.
I'm going to leave behind all I know.
I'm going to run into the forest.
I am done being the star of this show.

134

Iris Levin

gray morn

lifting her heavy head
from night's wet pillow
she sits in silence
spreading her veil
ghosting over a world
without sky land or sea
she shakes her blanket
over the morning
specks of light flare
exposing the night's secrets
and the day's possibilities

Silently
The beauty in the gray
Lost in mists of fog
Mysterious
The world without sky, land, ocean
She shakes her
She visits often
She sits in silence
Ghosting over the water
She is the gray ghost
Fog is the gauzey sea's breath
She envelopes
The clouds descended and concealed the world
she spread her veil over the morning
She smothers

Elise Levitt

At One

It doesn't begin a thing,
This first o'clock;
Existing mid stride towards a cubicle
Or passes, unnoticed,
While fending off centaurs
And dream beasts.
It becomes the real myth.

One is not a pivot point.

I was already walking
When my foot touched down,
And by the time
We saw the moon
First impressed
There were already
Handprints all over
Every inch of space between
Here and there.

It is nothing once,
When you have passed,
Ah ha
When you have gone,
Ah ha.

Life is so many legendary

One o'clocks;
Discovering you've laced your shoes,
Or that you've lined your face
With extra knowing.

Janine Logan

Worn Love

Our love is worn out
Tattered by events
An unheard heartbeat
Washed away

Our love stopped growing
We stopped relating
But we robotically carry on
Time ticks away

We muddle through the mediocrity
Hopeful, there is a chance
It's unlikely, now
Dreams carried away

Our children prosper
Despite our stagnation
They are unaware, as are you
Love washes away

All promises are good intentions
I hold on to that
Despite reality's interference
We are led away

Sheri Lynn

Vaccine?

"Peace is not merely a distant goal that we seek, but a means by which we arrive at that goal."
– Dr. Martin Luther King Jr.

This virus, not Covid, the one
plaguing souls driven to feast
on fear, anger, intolerance, privilege...

Is there a vaccine to be made there?
Can social scientists, healers, artists collaborate,
find an antidote as fast as Pfizer conceived?

Or is it mirrors we seek?
Truth telling, no excuses accepted, to
implore excavation of truth from chicanery?

If such denial should burst free from malignant cells,
will waiting arms extend with open hearts,
or be crossed behind indignant armor?

Or will healing spring blooms burst forth
from many justice seeds planted in winter
by patient, persistent democracy heroes?

Or is it love?
Could it be so easy?
Do people know, they deserve love?

139

Would the virus be void of hosts
if accountability lifts equity to let peace
intent see beyond judgement's frown?

Would such vaccines soften hurts, fears, anger whips?
Will goodwill kernels that don't come from a needle
spark vast crucial healing grace anew?

John Lysaght

Word Mining

I am beside myself
Trying to get motivated,
But nothing happens---
Complete hollowness.
I can hear the echo
Of my words
As they reverberate
Locked in place.
My creativity abandons me
To a desert of cliches.
Inspirational fatigue
Has me at a standstill---
Amorphous words and phrases evaporate,
As I slog through stale vocabulary
Leaving me as an empty vessel---
Thought sterile.
I stare at wordless pages,
As my blank mental canvas
Haunts—no---taunts me.
I grope for signs of life.

Tomorrow, I will hope and wait
For a reprieve---
For an end to my stagnation--
Rescued by a re-fertilized imagination.

Mikayla Lyston

Orange and teal

"Orange and Teal" I say in my head..
Orange and Teal..
orange and Teal..

Your favorite colors.
I must remember these colors.

You see, I worry I might forget these colors.
I always remind myself.
"Orange and Teal"

Although a small detail,
It's major one to me.
It allows me to see you in new shades.

My world went from
black and white to
Orange,
Teal,
Red,
and Blue.

Orange and Teal.
A unique combo yet a beautiful combo.
Perfectly, describing you.

Orange and Teal.
A perfect summer evening
Tasteful and wonderful..

My two new favorite colors to add to my list.
Orange and Teal.

Joan Magiet

Because You're Late

I stare at clouds streaked gold
by sun coloring the horizon.
Electric sounds from a party disrupt
my forced attempt to shape a poem.

I sip a martini on the restaurant terrace,
dab a spill with a crumpled napkin.
A metaphor bleeds into whiteness.

Hands on my watch join
at fifteen minutes before the next hour.
I think into another martini
surrounded by gravel cries of seagulls
in skyward design exploring Oyster Bay,
now dressed in twilight
like trees in a Blakelock painting.

Children decorate the shore,
speak in shrill staccato syllables,
toss pebbles at waves,
that bend into foam circles,
fade on wet sand,
first whole, then half,
as I...

Nicholas Malerba

Plea

I am Earth
Save my trees!
Please don't
Pollute my sea's
Plea for help

I am Earth
Trees green
As a recycling bin
Use one please!

My grass is green as emeralds
Help!
Plea for help

My sea's are deep blue
My branches soar high in the sky
Help me please!
Plea for help

I am Earth

I am Earth

Cristian Martinez

Beyond Walls of Confinement

Yesterday I walked outside into the garden in search of safety.
Closed doors surround me but the sweet aroma fills my senses.

The innocence of daisies and tulips
are being reborn for butterflies to gather.

Blackberries are ripe and ready to be savored,
their juices exploding in my mouth.

Blue jays and mockingbirds sing beautiful songs,
nature's voice is heard.

What I need the most is the sand beneath my toes,
running through tall grass with my friends,

a world that seems unheard of now.

I wish for a tomorrow of new beginnings where everyone
can gather socially in colorful fields of existence.

Michael McCarthy

After the Yard Work

Looking outward
and inward
while sitting on a lawn chair
in the afternoon shade
listening to the music of my youth
on my nifty iPad
gathering thoughts
writing a poem
sipping cold water.

A butterfly
or was it a moth
darting back and forth
with seeming abandon
in my backyard.

Or could its
frantic flight
have been
fraught with purpose.

Disappearing
beyond the puffy hydrangeas.

Suddenly surprised by this gnat
buzzing around my left wrist
while the birds, unseen
continue to sing away.

by myself
so I thought.

Rosemary McKinley

Beach Circle

Each day we stake our beach sand claim
Blue and green striped umbrellas with matched chairs sit close by
One couple starts speaking to another
Next day, we are looking to sit nearby
Sharing drinks, soda, and chips
 Talking, laughing
Enjoying the silver, sparkly view of the bay
As the days move on, some jump up to settle the boats
For those stopping in the sand
We exchange "hellos"
Extending our circle to include
More and more children and adults
Laughter and good will abounds

Some come by land, some by sea
All arrive at our designated spot
To visit with newfound friends
Keeping the rule of the day,
 laughing and sharing drinks and snacks
reminding me of my childhood days
in the 1950's
at the Sea Cliff Pavilion
where other families found friends and enjoyed
their place in the sun

Janet McLaran-Wade

Zeus

Oh! Great Zeus; god of the skies, lightning and thunder
Whirling your lightning bolts like toys, telling gods and mortals to surrender
On Mount Olympus you reign triumphantly
And as the king of gods you rule the skies courageously

Overthrowing your father Cronus put you on the map
Showing your ruthlessness and knowledge, confirmed you didn't care who you zapped
To protect your siblings to escape father's cannibalistic trap
You deemed yourself the youngest and the eldest of the lot

And, taking victory over the Titans was just another feat
Like releasing the family from prison, disgrace and defeat
Dividing the world among your siblings was the best you could do
Choosing the skies to master was an honor, just showing what luck was about
The other gods describe you with omnipotent powers
But your sexual appetite completely reduced and denounced

Oh Zeus! You embrace many titles and authority
Making you a controversial individual ruling society
A man of power! Lacking sexual dignity
Yet, still a prominent figure in
Greek Mythology

Gene McParland

Absolute Stillness of Movement

Standing on the shoreline,
night surrounds me;
glistening lights
out in the darkness.
I wonder
do butterfly dances
out there in the night?

There's a unity here,
no boundaries
between sky and ocean.

Out of the stillness
breaking waves sing to me.
The night air tastes so sweet.

Perfect peace.

Ria Meade

Balancing Act

I walk through this space called life, arms straight out:
    to the left, to the right, a bird in flight, a tightrope act,
    holding back time with the left hand,
        catching tears in my cupped right one.
Sometimes, my arms complain how heavy the challenges they carry are;
    other times, their burden is lightened by helping hands.
Our legs should be strong to carry us.
    In case one falters, its partner remains.
Our head is central to guide every muscle, fiber, bone, nerve, breath;
    the brain orchestrating their functions, keeping body's rhythm:
        a bird in flight.

When first negotiating this new, dark life,
    my arms flapped with fatigue,
        my legs faltered underneath me.
        Fear visited, then took a seat. Doubt followed suit.
Remembering prayers, I chose words of my own:
    Doubt, shame, despair.

Treading through this darkness life suddenly had become,
    I began to hear sounds that eventually led me forward.
        Accepted hands outstretched, feeling for purchase.
When faith began walking with me—or I began to walk with faith—
    I allowed myself to trust the ability to balance the pain
        of the unknown ahead.
    Finding courage within, I was able to take the next step.

I still walk this space called life, darkness accepted.
    Had thought balance was my arm's job;
        The left weighed low by age, illness, loss, all that time brings us.
        The right arm allowing for the run-off:
            anger, regrets, depression, failures, release in tears.
But is it my heart's job too, I wonder,
    as I precariously balance on my high wire tonight?

No matter how even-keeled I felt only hours ago,
    I heard a sound that toppled everything—
—a noise I'd heard before and not understood,
because it wasn't my own.
But now understanding another's balance was in jeopardy,
    I recognize how many similar souls need to learn
        to move forward with courage.
Each life finds its own space to walk through,
    whether in light or challenged without it.
        I am not the only one seeking balance on life's high wire.
        I am not the only bird in flight.

Alice Melzer

120 Days and Nights of Contrast

The Mythical bird's ability to calm the seas weakened.
After Halcyon Days, snows fell in wet, soft clusters.
Winds grasp nests as quick as lightening.
And dash them down onto the ground.
Along with them go heavy, ice coated branches.

Small animals scurry into secluded spaces.
Woe befalls the slow, less sharp eyed, and older creatures.
Mortals, as possible, retreat indoors; doing what they do.
Yet not all plans prove peaceful.

After January's Cold Moon, temperatures rise.
Snow shoveling folks dare to uncover what lay below.
Crystals dangle from trees and shimmer seductively.
Swiftly elves hid the tree's tiaras.
Lest their dazzling cause lust, envy, and theft.

Across the bay, ice shifts, cracks, and sometimes moan.
February's Fog, the elusive prestidigitator, works a soft white cloak.
It rolls lissome, supple, and surrounding all in a hush tones.
It hides the miscontent of ogres and oligarchs.

Beneath the Hungry Moon, owls and eagles hunt.
Another raptor readies and meets with resistance.
In a blur, Sharp-shinned-hawks swoosh.
Some disappear into the flurry of feathers and fur.
Woe to the innocent, weak or enfeebled.

Under the Snow Crust Moon, flurries fly, into the Ides of March.
Below the frozen ground, roots harbor; seeds prepare.
In softer, brown earth worms roust and snowdrops flower.
Purple crocuses dance to delight Persephone.

Equinox divides the invisible lines and worries continue.
120 days and nights of nature and disturbing news.
Heeding Mars, Ares, adds the Virus's sour fruit into a vat.
Will Chaos drink, drunk with power, can War be abated?

In early April, moss brightens and grows green.
Blood cries of tyrants could freeze before summer comes.
Mortals too close to the precipice, could halt or fall.

Lisa Diaz Meyer

Old Neighborhood

I could tell
It was an old neighborhood
As I sat on the fire escape
There wasn't much action
Only children playing games
Dilapidated cars lined the streets
Houses, old and broken,
Looked as if life were nonexistent
Yet from the windows
Clotheslines sloppily draped
The neighbor's laundry
Rusted garbage cans were twisted
And bent with age and abuse
A man appeared from behind a tree
His face and movements, drained
Then, I recognized him
This was our landlord
Who has lived here
For most of his life

Rita Monte

Apology to an Octopus

Poem inspired by "My Teacher the Octopus" Documentary- Won Academy award 2021

Dear octopus
when I was a little tot
i liked to eat you a lot

you were tasty sweet and yummy
oh so delicious for my tummy

my friend rolls her eyes at the restaurant
she says, don't eat that octopus
order a croissant

and now when I see you on the plate
I'm so sorry for your tragic fate

i learned
you have two hearts and nine brains
Blue blood runs in your veins

Royalty you are for sure
camouflage
survival
so much to endure

intelligent
curious and playful too
in the future I shall no longer
eat you

without further ado…
waiter, please
I think I'll have
the beef stew

CR Montoya

Tapestry

When our children were little
their day ended with a story.
With a well-worn book in hand,
an adventure ensued.
Rereading a tale prompted a declaration - -
Again!
though, after a moment,
our child would reengage.
It got so that this became a game
as memorized words sprouted from eager minds.

While time-honored fables never grew old,
I found myself wanting to travel new roads.
At times these sojourns were adaptations,
though more often
the words were plucked from the clouds.

When I think about those improvised journeys
I try to recall one, though it seems
they are hidden from daylight.

Now all five children have nests of their own,
some with willing participants.
    one thing remains constant,
Storytime!

One day while visiting our daughter,

Storytime arrived.
that wonderful interlude
when dreams are made
and eyelids grow heavy.

Like a spy, I tiptoed up to listen.
As an original narrative was weaved,
words, like water flowed
from our daughter's fertile imagination.

Unfamiliar sentences harkened back
to a time when our children were young,
eyes were as big as moons,
and sleep came with a kiss and a smile.

What a wonderful end
to our grandchild's day,
and a grand surprise gift for me.

Kim Mortensen

House Sale

When you see a sale you
should be with my family
to go check it out.

You can get a lot of things
at a sale like a chair.

You say you don't need
anything but you come out
with a lot of stuff!

Glenn Murphy

The Park

I ring your phone, you answer my call
Wanting to know if you wanna play ball
We pick a time, settle on four
There's five of us now, soon to be more

We all go in looking for others
We may go on our separate ways
We all come out as sisters and brothers
But none of us will forget these days

Man with a guitar makes the scene
A slice of life, all in our teens
We gather together, everyone's there
We choose up sides, you check your hair
Converse kicks, well-worn jeans
Restless hearts, unspoken dreams
Original sin, coming of age
Our story of life, not sure what page

Everyone needs a place in the sun
To contemplate life, decide what to share
A place to turn to, a place to run
That's the reason we show up there

We sit around, shoot the breeze
Stake our claim from beneath the trees
Too tall grass and azure skies

Basketball hoops, short goodbyes
Playing it cool so no one would know
Secretly hoping a certain someone would show
So many laughs, some trepidation
Different paths, same destination

It matters not, bad or good
We come together from the neighborhood
Before the light, after dark
To the place we simply call 'the park'

Ed Nardoza

An American Tunes In

The news is back on;
Again it's not looking good.
Neon-vested volunteers
Are searching for signs of life
In piles of rubble
On the other side of the world,
Smoke clinging to what's left
Of a two-story structure
With upstairs vanity
And mirrors exposed,
An open-sided infinity.
A forever's forever.

Add up the absolutes
To corner a conscience,
A sense of the senseless,
As if the mathematics
Of a feeling might give it
More heft, or believability.
This is real, not a dream.
And what's your proof?

Doesn't randomness
Tell us anything?
Just what you want it to tell you.
Like in quantum's crazy mechanics:

Anything that can happen
Will happen.

More a troubled melancholy
Than a madness, then.
For the keeper of that flame,
A mis-read Van Gogh,
The wan, the imperfect,
The desultory, the abject
Were messengers of the divine,
As much as the skyward cypress,
Iris-blue-gold field
And stunted undergrowth,
Redemption a one-size-fits-all proposition.

How then does one categorize
A knowingly wrongful act?
How to convey such a scene?
One can't be too mindful
Of losing control and going off
Or it won't be believable.
More likely it's found in
Subtle disparagement,
The psychic equivalent
Of a quiet drinker
Internalized in a corner,
With limited liability,
Conscious of how quickly
A blithe voice lightens things up
Before turning down.

Staying up for the weather and sports,
Nudged toward the group dynamic.
We must call today while supplies last;
We must customize our car insurance;
We must ask our doctor
If the peculiar new drug is right for us;
We must brace for an approaching storm system,
Umbrellas colorful and in working order.
After another short break
We'll get all the highlights
Of who won and who lost.
We'll be right back, they said.
Stay with us.

Valerie Nifora

O' Tide

O' tide
Flow through
Catch me
Let me not fall.
The heaviness
It bears down
To carry all.
Come
Embrace me
Lull me off to sleep.
I offer
This broken heart.
It's yours
To keep.

George H. Northrup

Audience

"Oh Bob," she cried, "don't kill yourself,"
improvising drama from his feigned
impatience at the curb.
He teetered in a moment of suspense
above those cliffs of peril
as a smoking dragon passed
and pulled into a stop.
Then, like a knight in rapture
at the Holy Grail,
he bowed in mannered chivalry
and offered her his arm.

Amused to see this urban slapstick,
I watched from several feet away.
"Don't think this beard was always tweed,"
I'd like to say, already feeling old,
"this aspect settled and serene."
Seeing her in baggy coat and tennis shoes,
I thought of bell-bottom jeans
and psychedelic marches on the Pentagon,
a previous millennium to them.

As Phlebas the Phoenician fades
and my Polonius emerges slowly now,
I miss the animation I would need
to parry their performance
with equal action of my own,

now so earnest and so temperate
I would risk their prompt dismissal
as a fool.

Mark C. Nuccio

A Natural Deed

Heard a feverish chirping
In dark, dead hours of night
When birds are usually silent.
And silence is a sleeper's delight.
.

I wondered what the commotion
could possibly be about.
I promised that come the morning
I would try to figure it out.
.

When the sun had fully risen
I walked to the nearby woods
There I found a brown sparrow
Dissected and dead on the ground.
.

I looked towards the higher limbs
Of the dense surrounding trees
And soon spied a Great Horned Owl
With evidence of the sparrow's demise
Displayed on his great grey breast.
.

It was then I fully understood
The nights chirping was not a serenade
But the sparrow's desperate appeal
In desperation and fright
For rescue, comfort, and safety.
As the Great Horned owl swooped down

In the deep, dark dead of the night.

.

I felt sorrow for the little sparrow
Yet no anger toward the Great Horned owl
For she had committed a natural deed
To fill her inbred natural needs

.

And that was all there was to it.

Gracie Conway Panousis

As You Lay Dying

Things I Did
1. I sat in the saggy gray recliner provided by the ICU department for three never-ending, extremely short days sleeping off and on, my eyes opening and closing as if connected to strings held by some hateful controlling god
2. When others arrived, I ran home, showered, ate and returned chanting a mantra the entire time - please don't let me miss it please don't let me miss it, but how can you miss something you're hoping won't happen?
3. I played Words with Friends on my cell phone.

Things I Didn't Do
1. I didn't climb onto the bed and lie next to you.
2. I didn't stroke your sweet, dear face, trace your black eyelashes, soothe your hot forehead, and review our life together
3. I didn't play Layla or The First Time Ever I Saw Your Face to you
4. I didn't put lotion on your beautiful hands even as I shuddered at the memories of them whispering across my body
5. I didn't murmur, it's okay to go, we'll be all right. Rest now.

And Excuses
1. I was numb, in denial, shaking my head, feeling nothing but ... what?
2. I didn't know I only had three days

So Why Now?
1. Because I redo those three days every single day since
2. This time, I climb right into your hospital bed and wrap my body around yours, caressing your face and kissing your perfect eyebrows
3. This time, I press my lips to yours, giving you my breath, my soul I play our music, reminding you of those otherworldly private moments
4. This time, I tell you that you are my sole life's partner, my soulmate and I explain how sorry I am. I ask for forgiveness.
5. This time, I thank you for teaching me what love between a man and woman truly is.

Marlene Patti

Choices

We make choices everyday
some good
some bad
some nourishing
some fantastic, mind blowing
relieving, fulfilling
altering truths...

I didn't choose you though
you came to me
you saw your opportunity
you went in innocently
gently, meticulous
unrevealing, cautious...

It set me free to see
the shell of a woman I came to be
so docile so timid
I had lost my wild and free nature
because I was loved carelessly...

You helped me believe in me again
you encouraged me to see my reality
and because of you I exist
so fervently, passionately...

Such lavish thoughts made me see
why you chose me...

Mary C. M. Phillips

Mistakes

Dear Mistakes,

I didn't like you the first time we met and nothing has changed.

Please stop visiting me whenever you feel like it and reminding me that you exist, as you've become boring and frankly...predictable.

Everyone needs to reinvent themselves at some point and that goes for you too. Here's an idea: wear a costume henceforth. Maybe a costume in the form of a lesson. Yes, that's it, dress like a lesson! That would look good on you.

In fact, the next time you visit, I will make sure to only open the door if you're wearing your new "lesson" costume. Otherwise...you can't come in.

This is my house and these are my rules.

Your former host,

Mary

Kelly Powell

Grapes and the Relief of the Apocalypse
after Abstract World#2

this is not an evangelical
but early christians had a problem
when the end of the world did not come

they didn't want it to come
they just kept saying it and saying it
until people finally gave up

and said okay, okay it's coming
but there are these mouths to feed
and fishes to turn into loaves

and rheumatism and laundry
always more and more and more
laundry to fold and wash and fold

and wash and fold
and wash and fold
and they moved our favorite rock
where the women used to gather

together in community
to wash our clothes and gossip
and talk about the end of the world

and everyone's comings and goings

and perhaps talk a little treason amongst
the linens, the fine and not-so-fine

mixed together into one
dystopian heartache that would lead
to another and another so okay, the world

will be ending soon, until then take off
those filthy socks, so we can wash them
at our new spot, down river

Pearl Ketover Prilik

Since you split my lip

I learned that blood
really does taste like copper
pennies and that it is
possible for you to cry
copious tears in my lap
as I hold your hand and
notice that your knuckles
are swollen around small
cuts where my teeth hit
Since you split my lip
I dry your tears with a
dishtowel – suck the
blood back down my throat
and get you ice for your
too fast fist
and – No, there
is no need for sorry
because I truly do
know that this time
will
be
the
last

Alexander Radison

Mourning Diary

"Like a bursting bubble: the realization that she no longer exists,
she no longer exists, totally and forever."

—Roland Barthes

Energy cannot be destroyed, only transferred,
or converted from one form to another.

The chemical energy of a stick of dynamite
converts to the kinetic energy of the explosion.

Or, a simpler example:
the energy from a thrown bowling ball is transferred

to the pins, sending them flying.
Humans are made of matter, but energy

is our lifeforce.

The chemical energy of digestion,
the thermal energy warming our blood,

the potential energy of us at rest
and its expression—the kinetic energy of motion,

all cease after death.

But that energy is not destroyed.

It goes somewhere. Turns into something else.

Maybe, our body's energy
transfers to the soul, sending it flying

out into the universe like those bowling pins,
our essence moving through space in perpetual motion, free

of the body's mechanical limits.
Barthes is wrong. She still exists, somewhere.

She exists.

Phil Reinstein

Cancel Culture

Cancel this cancel that cancel culture is where we're at
cancel culture doesn't do it for me
cancel high cancel low cancel popular TV shows
 cancel culture has caller ID
 if I need to stay in your good graces
 I'll stay away from your safe spaces
cancel near cancel far cancel *Fox* and *NPR*
cancel culture cannot cancel me

Could a book should that look make me shudder get me cooked
cancel culture can be so scary to me
here and now I avow cancel culture has somehow
caused quite a controversy
those old black and white movies still make me feel groovy
love's sweetest songs are treasures you see
give a shout hear me out as of now there is no doubt
cancel culture cannot cancel me

When I am sad and alone *Facebook* comes to my phone
Tik Tok and *Twitter* tag along too
 I put my trust in big tech now I just must double check
Wikipedia and *Google* could both be untrue

I'm bemused quite confused feeling faint needing booze
'cause I'm camping in a new campground
so obtuse I can deduce have matured have been seduced
book burning no longer out of bounds

working as cancelers are the most reasonable folks
ego driven chancellors who just can't take a joke
let's call a truce cut me loose call my doctor Dr. Seuss
cancel culture is out there cancel culture needs repair
cancel culture cannot cancel me

Diana R. Richman

Impermanence

Cycles, seasons, stages of life
Change, transformation
Freeze, flight, or fight

Being born, dying, phases of life
Transition, journey
Fear, or invite light

Enjoy, suffer, slivers of life
Strengthen, weaken
Face, or out of sight

Collect, let go, choices in life
Create space, clutter
Forge, or seek night

Live now, be present, throughout your life
We don't last forever
No matter your might

Relax, accept, this need not make sense
That our life here on earth
Is impermanent.

Allie Rieger

Ponderosa

With new eyes
I see your old soul.
So pine forest strong,
deafening the sounds
of my crashing waves.
Lunar controlled.
Needles.
Instruments of suicide
turned organic
around your roots.
Finally able to
decompose naturally.
Chemical controlled.

John Robilotta

Commuting

The going on and going on
gets to me.

The years.
A flash.

A drag.
The jolting,

slogging
never ending of it.

Life is like this train.
Hours coming and going,

always winding up
at the same place.

The faces on the train change,
or remain the same.

But I keep getting
on.

Rita B. Rose

Winter Creeper

Winter Creeper you are strong as I am
gay and green nothing stands in your way
you fight in summer for the right to thrive
your legacy clings upon a *stone wall,* unchanged

Gay and green nothing stands in your way
horticultural heretics neglect your imprint
your legacy clings upon a *stone wall,* unchanged
no matter how they try to sever you—you cling

Horticultural heretics neglect your imprint
Emerald Gay Winter Creeper adhere to the wall
no matter how they try to sever you—you cling
forever living and climbing the *stone wall*

Emerald Gay Winter Creeper adhere to the wall
you fight in summer for the right to thrive
forever living and climbing the *stone wall*
Winter Creeper you are as strong as I am

Patricia Rossi

Sea Shells

Fine white china smashed
Jagged fragments haphazardly
    dot the shore

Collected keepsakes, tucked
in summer short pockets, tossed in
    plastic sand pails

Beach treasures donned in faint
echoes….. rhythmic laps
    of an ocean roar

A A Rubin

Arse Poetica

My poetry is all amiss—
My meter's off,
My rhyme's a mess:

My metaphors' irregular,
Round pegs enjambed rectangular—
My similes are like…well…fails;
Is there a cure to fix what ails—

This limpid, languid, lacking verse?
(Alliteration, it's the worst)

I cannot write oh dear, oh dear!
I've lost my muse, it's clear, I fear

I trip all o'er my metric (al) feet
Which makes my lines sound…incomplete—
My stresses have me stressing out
And though I can't forget about (it)

My rhymes they slant so far they fall,
I should have left them in the vault.

A cesura here—to interlope
Is there a volta soon? I hope—

Or is there nothing in these lines,

Snaked 'round each other, serpentine—
Contorted for the sake of craft,
Devoid of meaning, choked and daft—

Howbeit now, what's past is past—
We've reached the end, alas—at last.

Brion Ryder

Conversation On 25 A, November 1987

I (A)

I take him, arms supporting
a withering scarecrow as an
orderly slowly moves the wheelchair away

my father leans on me like a rusted bicycle,
tires flat against the weathered south wall
of a lonesome, abandoned barn

slow slump into the rear seat of an old Ford,
no longer capable of riding shotgun
in the only car he has ever known

II

there is no apprentice program
or manual with appendix
numbered illustrations
outlining steps in precise terminology
mislaid glossary for the
language of life, love, a
definition of stage four,
proxy,
table of contents omitted
to complete the lexicon,
where the magnitude of

a single day
could be scribbled in the
margins

III

he would say this to me:
"will you please lose that damn Brooklyn accent"
but there are things we cannot disavow
like the dirt that clung to his skin
born in fields of corn, rye that swayed
the way a mother rocks her child to sleep
and I was the son of a farmer
too soon to cultivate the earth

I (B)

it is a long road home
navigating through a weald of wildwood
where roots that run deep
covered in pine mulch
crisp yellows, browns, reds
tall timber preparing for another
cold dark dance

I did not recognize the need for
silence…
spoke of land we planned to purchase
rear view mirror catches
a glimpse of sullen eyes
locked in that hollow

gaze of regret. There, in a whisper,
close to tears, I strained to listen,

"there has been a change of plans."

Pat Gallagher Sassone

Sea Secrets

My finger like an artist's brush draws each letter
in the sand
A word, a line
joy and anguish,
a silent shout out pulled away by
a wet wild wave while
the wind whispers across the sea.

Robert Savino

Illusion of Time

"We are living in a culture entirely hypnotized by the illusion of time."
~ Alan Watts

There's an emptiness that lies ahead for everyone.
I've seen it in dream fragments of imagination.
The numbers 9 & 3 sag from a melting clock,
creating a parenthesis effect around the 6.

The second hand loosely swings like an untimely
pendulum with little energy left in its battery.
Flesh digits are stitched from shards of denial
where steady hands had set to work for years.

A path is brightened only by stars.
A voice is heard from a dusty bookshelf.
And pointing into the misty mirror image
of a perfumed room, I hardly recognize myself.

This dream is unlikely to outlast a grandfather clock,
while the young, live-streaming through internal channels
identify me with the haunting of a cuckoo clock,
not aware of what will pass before them.

From this I've learned . . .
never to ask what time it is.

Karen Schulte

Alchemy

They stand next to each other in this old photograph,
separated by inches exactly the same from top to bottom
as if tailor made by an invisible marker. They look
straight at the camera, smiling and proud in their
best clothes waiting for a celebration.

That is how I remember them, side by side,
never touching, at least never seen by me.
At home, even their beds were narrow twins
with a night table and two lamps between,
a bedroom for roommates not a long-married couple.

My grandfather, tall and slim,
handsome with a shock of white hair.
Grandma, at his side, short and round,
never at a loss for words, in Yiddish
or any other language she could muster.

They seem to have lived in two separate worlds
while together in one: there was some rumor
their marriage was an arrangement. It may have
been so but they appear to be content.

Whatever they had, it was more than they
bargained for at a time when there was no way
of knowing what lies ahead when you
cross an ocean as wide as the Atlantic.

But here they stand posed together
as inexplicable as if they landed on Mars
flung from some dying planet
to a place they could never imagine—

where a sideways glance and grit could turn dross
to gold or an ordinary stone to something like marble.

Sophia Schiralli

Poetry Dripping

When the poetry stops
when it just drips from the pot
that's when you need to give more
more tears, more sweat
slave harder away, keep watching
the water, be patient my dear
be patient
and pray that you'll hear the music once more
before all your days pass to nights
and the ground is your floor.
and I don't know much,
but I know this to be true-
If you keep on going,
you'll be king before noon
then you'll gladly keep on going,
it's the spirit in you
so, please keep on going

Jacqueline Shortell-McSweeney

Sailing Away

Under morning's glowering sky,
John bends to his visions, washes sails, and stitches,
fights needle through stiff canvass;
Drops woman's thimble and pricks finger
---Blood for the sails!

Seaman's precision takes old cotton
seam by seam from worn planks and works in a gentle hand,
setting sturdy cloth in place,
line by line, dream by dream.
Sailor's eyes on the horizon,
he caulks hull's fearless wood in final seal --with a love one gives to family.

In the church light of old barn
the unfrocked mariner performs sea rituals.
Mast and rudder sanded to fresh wood.
Male sweat mixes turpentine and varnish.
Daughters and son run up and down ladders
to offer swipes of paint for pride of the Ship.
Far offshore, Neptune and Nereids wait
as children share blue water prayers with their Odysseus,
a moment,
in this slanting shed.

Then the Siren sings.
Tied to the mast of her sweet-sounding lust,
John is mad for Javea, Cefalu, and Patmos.

He rolls charts,
lays in the stores and storm gear.
He checks the lines, knots, and splices,
fills the running lights with kerosene,
rubs brass lamps till the stars shine.
His wintered dreams ready to sail.
This night,
Circe will lead him from the confines of the bay,
This night,
the moon will weigh anchor.
This night,
Memory will leave quotidian shore.

But, oh the wide-beamed ship, trapped
between tall rock of Scylla and whirlpooling Charybdis,
Blameless children against a raging Penelope,
This night,
You never leave the cat-tailed bay for the sea.

The wood boat sits in my backyard,
cutting through choke weed.
The hull rots to the land,
a playground for his grandchildren.
And this, sorrow's song to my father,
                    who would not sail from us.

Keith Simmons

Shutdown Stay At Home Poetry Time

these poets on Zoom come stepping into the room
they sign up for the mic and the lights go down
don't make the intro too long   we want to hear your poem
I send a smiley face or a wishful kiss

she reads "oh baby I'm yours" but I know she ain't mine
I turn the video off 'cause I tend to be shy
I'm filled with so many insecurities
on Zoom I'm only two dimensional
I used to be three

but how do they do this   how do they do that
they make the words come first and the lips move last
it's an inversion in time or a perversion of rhyme
it's the shutdown stay at home poetry time

I read "oh maybe I'm yours" she says "you're out of your mind"
then she turns down the lights and pretends to be shy
I'd like to be with her in her poetry room
but she's a virtual lady in a virtual Zoom

yes the words come first and the lips move last
how do all these hours go by so fast
it's an inversion in time   it's a possible crime
it's the shutdown stay at home poetry time

Leslie Simon

The Envelope

she enters the testing room
the written part of the teaching exam

old insecurities walk in beside her
her secret of feeling not smart enough follows her in

four years of college didn't prepare her
she's drowning in her fear of failure

heart racing, pulse pounding, eyes blurring
she's one of the last to finish

dreadful way to spend her birthday
but maybe it would bring her good luck

winter months are cold and unkind
as is her confidence. She waits!

the rest of her life depends on this one test
terrified she'd fail, her secret would be found out

the door that could open to a career
depends on some words on a piece of paper

afraid to open the envelope when it arrives
she prays "surprise me" "surprise me" "surprise me"

petrified, she stares ahead, sees nothing
frozen in the cosmos, she's sinking

her peripheral visual shrinking in darkness
anxiety tormenting her senses

perspiration drips
hands clammy

finally tearing open the envelope, she's relieved
grateful her prayers were fulfilled

her self-esteem, now elevated
her confidence now repaired

feeling less than…was yesterday
today she looks ahead at the possibilities

for tomorrow begins
a celebrated career

Emily-Sue Sloane

Open Mic

Just three narrow stairs
separate stage from audience
at the Northshore Original Open Mic
at Finley's in Huntington
Some folks sprint to the mic as their turn comes,
others travel a slightly more hesitant path
guitars slung over shoulders
mandolins tucked under elbows

The host introduces each artist
with words of friendship and gratitude
drawn from his deep well of kindness

Deft fingers scale frets
of Guilds, Martins, Taylors
rich in woody hues and timbre
The tunes carry tales of love
   lost, found, unrequited
protests and politics,
bars, cars, and trains—lots of trains
Worldly and other-worldly wonders
spun like shimmering threads
into the songs

Occasionally, a voice cuts through the din—
the chatty bar crowd in the back takes a listen
Applause rolls through the room
as each song fades to silence

For the ones who are game,
and the ones there to witness,
trust builds, worries melt away
Hope returns
coaxed alive by the music

Lynne D. Soulagnet

Connetquot River Inlet

If you stretch you can see
past the branched trees
where they congregate
before they swim further out
away from the nebulous
lines of property where water
laps upon the shore

Feathers of downy white
reflect off rippled blue liquid
float like a symphony of notes
on a cloud of ivory, all beauty
grace and harmony

Some have paired, found mates
elongated necks held high, they
stay together, drift past reeds
so calming to catch sight
of them peacefully gliding
along the winding river

Until an arrow pierces the air
arcs, misses its intended target
deliberately cruel child's play
I wait for another, hold my breath
but it does not come, not on this day

Ivy Sommer

587

Sparingly and Lavishly
Sparingly and lavishly went into a store
Sparingly was happy with nothing, but lavishly wanted
more
Sparingly and lavishly went to a gala party
Sparingly ate nothing, while lavishly ate hearty
Sparingly and lavishly wanted to work out
Sparingly was quiet, while lavishly had to shout
Sparingly and lavishly went to a park
Sparingly had enough, while lavishly wanted to stay
until dark
Sparingly and lavishly went to a beach
Sparingly played in the water, while lavishly wanted to
teach
Sparingly and lavishly are very good friends
Sparingly and lavishly when together, are at opposite
ends.

Dd. Spungin

Blue

Because blue is missing from the sky
and silver silence has been broken by sharp noises
I paint with blue—
Because tragedy exacts my peace of mind
and worry suffocates my hope
I paint with blue—

Night gives succor and relieves the hurt
but morning comes in too-dim light
so paint with blue
The day, uncertain of its goal
The road already blocked by pain
so paint with blue—
Tomorrow, someone's yesterday,
already written in a history book
so paint with blue—

If sunshine comes and clears the sky
I'll know a hand has chosen blue
and I will bask
and I will bow
as skies once more are painted blue.

Ed Stever

At The Gym

Row after row
of stationary treadmills,
men, women, children,
all garbed in Adidas, Nike, Converse,
gazing up, entranced,
running pell-mell towards
the twenty flat screens
dangling from the corrugated ceiling,
each running a commercial_
all the runners hurtling forward
like Pavlovian dogs.

d w Stojek

Death at a Social Function

"Had Brad Thumbstock merely forgot?" a plausible oversight but how
could one account for the flush of his cheeks, pallid then hot,
upon witnessing Death awkwardly tripping over a loosened floorboard,
presumptively attending by foregone invitation:
a wilting Parabola affecting curtsy,
the reluctant courtesy married to the decay of perpetuity.
Engaging dilettantes and debutantes,
parley riddled with mundane staples: "What do you *do* for a living?" and
"Where to from here?"
Each interrogative responded to with withering
vulgarism and unwitting ultimatum
plied in a farce of mistaken identity: as the
bakelite Daisies were made to fade
in place of very viable Geraniums.

Popping and puncturing a piñata of popular epidemic, mere
Gossip flamed to character assassination;
Libel, at best: bitter grapes, since
Man upended Apes.
Hearsay figuring Death, after a fashion, agrarian: a scythe and cloak being as
last Season as the wheat of each passing Soul,
as rhinestones and worsted tulle.

Now, *de rigueur* preparation of a dead man's plate,
composed of gourmand hors d' oeuvres
speared through with gambrel picks;
medlar compote on quisling rye, amanita stuffed with hemlock; a
stale bagel smeared with lox the stuff of a diet and
appetite accompanying pox.
Distracted, the entourage errantly sets a dwarf in the metaged
casket of an ox,
the rattling as much a nuisance as the persistent Weed of Dives as
there is nothing much new in Luxembourg,
save the posture of those who die...

210

Lennon Stravato

Hometown

Pink Floyd in the tape deck
enough gas for the day
Don't know how you worship
but that was once my way

I measured youth in miles
from the village to the shore
I hear my rides are filed
inside of local lore

But at some point Eden slipped
from the rearview mirror's path
I don't think I know which trip
turned out to be my last

Today nostalgia drove me back
but I couldn't stay therelong
I'm on a different track
and singing my own songs

Fare thee well, my little town
we had our little patch of time
But don't call too often, now
you belong to younger minds

Jaishree Subramani

Let me be

Let me be the light that shines unperturbed
Hidden in a particle or a wave
Free to be straight, illuminating and undisturbed
Not trapped in crevices or cave

Let me be free to wander the universe so big
By physical laws tho bound
In harmony with quarks, leptons and the Higg
Despite the chaos around.

Let me be true and sincere to my natural state
And do what I'm meant to do
To find the right path and to illuminate
Happiness will follow through

Let me be unwavering in my love for life
Tho I'm deflected, bent or broken
Reclaim the energy from sorrow and strife
Or so the wise have spoken

Let me not color this world with rainbows great
Passing through life's prisms
We are just travelers in the journey of fate
Let's not fight about isms

Let me not judge and blame the other lights
Striving their best to be

Abandon scorn, anger and petty fights
Try some positivity

Let me try to make a brighter tomorrow
And the only way I could
Rise and shine with the others and grow
The end will be just good.

Let me realize why and from whence I came
A tiny source of light
Know that they, you and I are the same
A brilliance oh so bright

Let me evolve into a higher state of mind
The purpose of life it is
Marvel the strength and spirit of humankind
The only Life is this

Douglas G. Swezey

#1401 (Pins and Needles)

There has been much talk of it
Everyone has a theory
Speculation has reached back
Centuries, if not millennia
The Chinese have an ancient book
A cave moist with age called a centola
Cratered a manuscript, or parts of it
From the lost Mayan tribes
But even popes and bishops, Martin Luther
The Qur'an, Talmud, Bible
And the fringe groups as well
Have had it down in their
Desk planners as well
Arbour Day, Flag Day, Thanksgiving
Christmas, Armageddon

There have been many ways to prepare
I've seen the infomercials
To purchase TV dinners which decades last
And the specials about those who have
Turned underground bunkers or missile silos
Info functional, if not grey, storage
Facilities for life
After the great whatever it is that's coming

But it seems that's the point
I don't see the trees uprooting

To the sound of enormous zippers unfastening
There is no prickly pear
At five o'clock in the morning.
I recall the morning of 9/11
As one of the most quiet, serene
Picturesque dawning to break

What I fear is the whimper
The sigh
And then nothing

Nothingness

There will be no
Hour of darkness
Nor light either
No struggle
It will be just
So easy to give over
Into ablation

The sound of a pin drop
Would be as an earthquake
If there still
Were a pin
Something to quake

James Tucker

Unending Vow

A photo such as this
Deserves a lovely poem
For its fascination
My eyes begin to roam

A majestic setting sun
Is bowing beyond the trees
To the blessed star witness
Seeing all a Mother see's

Timeless it waits
Inviting you to look
Holding all the wonder
Of a classic story book

It must clearly be
The focal point of any room it's in
I'm sure minor kings will claim
To know the secret held within
But…

With such happiness
Beaming lovelier than the Sun
It is capturing the very moment
Two hearts becoming one

I am smiling with them now

Too impossible to contain
As I am drawn nearer
I am reflected in the frame

As my eyes look further still
The scales begin to fall
I am being allowed to see
This is no photograph at all

It's The masterpiece of an Unending Vow Between the Father bride and
man
Perfectly created by
The Holy artists hand

J R Turek

When We Met
for Joe Pantatello

It was summer, a Thursday night
and I was a bit nervous joining
a writing group I had heard about
but never summoned the courage
to go until then.

Spacious auditorium, a local library,
pleasant acoustics from my heels as I
made my way down to the front row
of plushy seats. I wanted to see and
hear everything, get to know the form
and function of the group before deciding
if I'd be coming back.

I put my pocketbook and tote bag
on the seat beside me, took out a journal
and pen. I was a little early so settled back
to wait for 7 pm. You were early too, took
a seat one away from me in that front row
that would become our regular seats.

I finished writing a line in a new poem
before it disappeared in a puff of remorse
and that's when you leaned across the seat
between us, and whispered words I will
never forget.

"I like your feet."

I smiled wide, my cheeks like apples
and thanked you. Almost 25 years later,
I remember what I was wearing. Toe rings
and ankle bracelets, white Candie slides
with silver and turquoise embellishments –
I still have them, think of you when I see them,
will keep them forever –
my feet summer-tan, my nails both hands
and feet painted with sailboats, sand castles,
blue skies, white clouds –
my usual summer artistry in polish.
We both chuckled, as though we knew
this would be the start of something
special and promising for years to come.

No courtship – I was in my early-thirties,
you early-seventies, perhaps avuncular,
our beginning. We expanded our meetings
to other workshops and readings, you
a prose writer, me primarily poetry;
in time, when your eyesight diminished,
me driving us for the evening meetings.

I am honored to this day that you
invited me to read at your book launch,
readings by your family only; and trusting
me to edit your stories, make suggestions
to improve from great to excellent. Oh,
how I treasure my autographed copy of
Robertson's Attic.

I talked about this poem for years,
we both laughed about its incarnation,
and now nearly 25 years later, you
have gone far beyond our horizons
to spread your angelic wings, and I,
finally, wrote the poem about
when we met.

I love you, Joe. I miss you.
Thank you for giving me this memory
to outlast eternity.
       Love, ~ Judy
Enjoy the journey...

Victoria Twomey

Rise Up and Sing

you will not know
that land beyond
from which it first took flight

nor who sent it
or how it came to be
inside your own sky

listen for the fluttering sound
of arriving wings
open the window

let it into your being
lead it to
your true-heart nest

if it wishes
before it leaves you
it will gift

one fragile
blue
speckled egg

that holds the sleeping words
of a folded poem
dreaming it is already born

with silence, with time
it will awaken
and emerge

open wide its wings
rise up into your sky
and sing

James P. Wagner (Ishwa)

Waterfall Wishes

I passed by a waterfall…
An indoor one, at a Casino…
A place I have been going to for over 20 years.
I took many trips there in my teens,
With my parents, before I could legally gamble,
And spent all my time at the arcade
That these escalators traveled to.
Up on one end,
Down on the other,
With this big, artificial, waterfall,
In the center,
Home to many coins,
Casino chips,
And arcade tokens…
Each one, representing a wish.
Quite a few,
I threw in there myself,
Back when the future was an infinite ocean…
Of what was possible,
Very few grooves carved yet,
Into the pathway of my life,
That couldn't be easily erased,
And tread over…

As I rode up this escalator,
Looking down again at the fall,
Seeing the water pass through the rocks,
Down to the big pool below…
I did my best to recall,
The desires of old,
Worthy enough of the price,
Of an expendable arcade token…
And a smile crept across my face,
As I realized,
Some of those wishes,
Had actually,
Come true.

Jillian Wagner

What Would I Do?

Having been an avid reader all my life,
I've often questioned what I'd do if I found myself in some of my favorite
books.
A spooky story?
Well, I enjoy a good scare, but I'll leave exploring the haunted house,
messing with the strange toys and hunting for crazed killers
to others because I like my head where it is, thank you.
But I'd probably be happy doing research on the sordid history of the town.
Well, provided that didn't put me on the killer's list.
Otherwise, the protagonists are on their own!
What about Redwall, a series I've loved since I was ten?
To be honest, I'm not really the adventerous type,
but I would totally join in the battles!
Now THAT sounds fun!
Then again, my point about liking my head where it is still stands...
Alright, then, what about the works of Roald Dahl?
I've loved his books since I was about three.
Well, I know how to cripple a leg, so that takes care of any witches.
I like chocolate, but if people start going nuts looking for golden tickets,
I would be content just sitting on the sidelines and watching the anarchy un-
fold
and buy Wonka bars on sale when the contest was over.
And should a giant piece of fruit fall from the sky?
I think I'd just roll my eyes at how the authorities handle the situation
and introduce myself as a neighbor later.
Yeah, that's what I'd do.
I'm cool not being a main character!

Pamela Wagner

One More Minute
For Patricia A. Sarica

I know I'm not the only one who has thought this,
When someone you know passes away,
But to only think if you had one more minute
To tell them that you are sorry for all the wrongs you did,
Now matter how small or big.
To I'm sorry it was you and not me,
To tell you how much you meant to me.
To say I would miss every phone call,
Just one more minute..

To say I wish I could have done something more.
To say I can't go on without you.
To say it will never be the same.

Days aren't as bright, nights are too long.
Holidays and birthdays are the saddest times.
To say, who knew you were a gift,
Lent to me, never to keep.
To say all the wisdom you shared with me,
All the lessons you taught me,
All the best you brought out in me…
I'm a shell of despair right now…
And I only wish I could tell you
For one more minute, that I love you.

Margarette Wahl

End Credits
for Francis Maiorino

When I saw the letters of your name
remember 9th grade health class
brought extra pens
just to loan you one,
you never came prepared.

When I saw the letters of your name
returned back to 1989
square-danced in gym class
your decision to moon the video camera
landed you in school suspension,
our gym teacher not amused, I was.

When I saw the letters of your name
reminded me of social studies class
you with a cold
acting scenes from *Godfather*
claiming you were Don Corleone
made me laugh, it still does.

When I saw the letters of your name
in the end credits of *Boardwalk Empire*
I gasped
smiled
proud to have known you
way back when.

When I saw the letters of your name
on Facebook,
it announced your passing
and arrangements of your funeral.
Gasp in disbelief still
I remember your influences on my life.
Love for Mob movies, Italians, Brooklyn…
I write a pen pal in Italy thirty years
all because of you.

Each influence with your memory I cling to
like every letter in your name.
Know there will never be another on this earth
unique and meaningful as you, Frankie.
Crush once a noun is a verb.

Herb Wahlsteen

Dirge

A tribe is strewn like sand on
a desert plain. Its oasis is dead.
Somehow, its oasis became a feast for
locusts. A long drought followed and
evaporated everything except sand and
people.

Futilely, the tribe tried to nurture seeds in the
countless miles of surrounding dunes.
Also, it tried to find meat, yet it found
only reptilian hearts and petrified
skulls. Choking gulps of mirages were drunk.

Soon, it became a feast for
preying lions and hyaenas, and
scavenging vultures and worms.

Now, all that remain
are bleached bones being
buried slowly by
sandstorms on
a desert plain.

George Wallace

Songs Of Love

I am like dark
　matter I live
in the factory
　I obey train
whistles
　I work all day
and earn
　my salt
in the
　anthracite
digging up
　death
to light
　the cities
　　of men
　and power
their terrible
engines;

　but at night
I walk out
into the
　darkness
to see
　what's
　　shaking
　among the

tombstones
and evergreens
  and party with the
    muses,
      all that
  fog
    dread
madness
    frenzy
curiosity
  can deliver;
  I party with
    the
    gone
generations
  and wish
I was free;

  that's when
    she comes to me
  the lady with eyes
like moon rockets
neck like oak and ivory
  with her
songs of love
half truths and
  utterly
    beautiful lies,
    songs
  no man
  may embrace;
dear lady
  these are the

songs
  only
   gods
and dreamers
   know
and the dead
fast asleep
in their naked
beds;

O stream
of eternal
forgetfulness
be slow
around my breast
  as you rise
help me
to remember.

Virginia Walker

Visitor
for Michael Walsh

May

I always talk to the dead
and perhaps I am already
in a silent dialogue with you,
although I am still struck
with the unreality of the news
delivered slowly by your mother.

Stunned I sit in my living room
and face the window of early May.
In the glass at eye level a glimmering
beauty looks in at me, beak straight.
"Michael," I cry out in a child's voice.
I want your spirit to be visiting me.

I feed the hummingbirds every year,
from May to September. They return
luminous, bearing in their plumage
the Caribbean as our azaleas bloom,
but this one knows me. I see Michael's
trickster-self departing on the air.

September

The visitor comes again to me
as what I must tell his family
gathered at his library memorial.
But how can I share with these
unknown of his kin, the sweet
spirit I knew him to be in all his living?

Finally, I speak of another world
In the stars, an island, where Michael
has settled. There in that ideal
of a child's imagination, he lives,
wearing a hummingbird mask.
Do I convince them of that place?

Michael, I cannot convince myself,
yet you visit me again in weekly turns
of your laugh, your impish cleverness.
My mother visits daily, my father
never so often. I am glad that you
  will fly at my eye in darting intervals.

Marq Wells

Confessions of A Vampire

Today I try to do things just a bit
differently than how we **used to do**
back In the Old Country.

For instance, I rise with the sun
and live life on the bleeding edge
by running through open spaces
with an asbestos blanket over my head.

Or, like this morning,
real food instead of blood.

Oatmeal with raisins and honey.
Beats having to hide the *bloody mess!*

and then just for kicks
I crushed a fortune cookie
and threw that in.

The Fortune? Ah... and this is *key*.

If you don't program yourself
Life will do it for you.

Lorraine Wodhanil

The Birth of a New Season

Oh the hue of the dahlias newly planted in the weather worn
soil of Winter's end.
There no purpose in one's digging of dirt but to draw
back the curtain and see the sun's spotlight reign on the stage
quieting the constant jabber of admiring passerbys
if only for a moment
A towering maple and oak, whose branches provide
the frame of a blue sky, sets the scene for a different forest
from cold months previous when they stood alone amongst
the foraging finch and snowy owl
The soft breath of a warmer breeze now welcomes the
gold finches and robins who fly above the deer
treading on the softened ground feasting
on tender shoots and newly formed grass preparing
for their fawns
The admiration of those who tread in this serenity
clear their minds of nonsensical clutter and obligatory
tasks put upom them in the hours before
There is no diligence in those to slow their pace,
just reveling in the virtual silence and the longing
to extend the peace

Jack Zaffos

Don't Try To Do Anything Special (Poetic Suggestions)

Don't try to do anything special.
It will enter you
when you open.
These words will seep within
and melt your heart.

Be open perhaps,
let the words come to you,
these words of loving strength.

Can you open your heart
and your ears to the words
of women and men
who spoke and wrote?

If you will accept them,
there is a baton
that is being handed.
Hold it humbly
For it contains the strengths
of holiness and love.

This is not a run for perfection,
we don't have the time for that.
Yet carry the baton

with the fullness of who you are,
the blemishes and the beauty,
for they are all one.

Steven Zaluski

Affection

An affectionate woman is good to find
and hold on to...
I'm like my Dad, after my Mom died so young and my wife did too...
All we search and long for is affection...
So hard to find, but it keeps us coming back for more...
Ladies hold the key to temptation and inspiration...
Be sweet and we'll come back forever...

Thomas Zampino

One Beat, One Measure, One Tear

One beat, one measure, one tear.

Our lives often seem little more than an experiment as we go first this way, then that. All the while looking for one unmistakable way forward.

Sometimes we find ourselves left behind, sometimes way out in front. Sometimes it's impossible to know the difference.

One beat, one measure, one tear.

We are not our mothers, we are not our fathers, we are not anyone before or to come. History is a guide, not a sentence. Tomorrow is a thought, not a cure. Treat today as you would a miracle. Because you already suspect that it is. Somewhere deep inside.

One beat, one measure, one tear.

About the Authors

Doug Abrams was born and raised on Long Island. After travelling a bit, and acquiring a bit of an education, he returned here to Long Island where he taught high school for 34 years before retiring to the life of a scholar poet.

Lloyd Abrams, a long-time Freeport resident, is a retired high school teacher and administrator and is an avid recumbent bicycle rider and long-distance walker. Lloyd has been writing short stories for over thirty years and poems for almost a dozen years. His works have been published in more than three dozen anthologies and publications. www.lbavha.com/write

Esther Alian is a Long Island based poet and writer. She has lived on 4 continents and her writing reflects the centrality of human experience transcending religion, culture and walk of life.

Sharon Anderson has been published in many international and local anthologies, has been nominated for a Pushcart prize, and has six publications of her own poetry. She serves on the advisory boards of the Nassau County Poet Laureate Society, co-hosts readings at Oceanside Library, and hosts the PPA poetry workshop at Farmingdale Library.

William H. Balzac is a poet and writer of fiction who resides in Deer Park, Long Island. He has been a contributor to the Bards Annual (2019, 2020, and 2021), and The Suffolk County Poetry Review (2019, 2020, and 2022). His latest collections of poetry can be found at Amazon (KDP) books/USA: "In The Days of Corona & New Poems," "Poems of Book & Writing Nights", and "Three Chapbooks."

Christine A. Barbour is descended from Adam Mott, one of the founding families of Hempstead, Long Island. She lives in Woodhaven, New York. In

2010, she founded *Iron Horse Poetry*, a free workshop, and currently facilitates its Facebook page. She tutored English and Math in the *Adult Learning Center* in the Elmhurst Queens Library. She holds an MFA in writing from Sarah Lawrence College and a BA from Queens College. Her poetry has been published in *Writer's Digest*, the *Bards Annual, the Nassau County Poet Laureate Society Review,* and the *Performance Poets Association, The Red Penguin Collection*, among others. Her inaugural book of poetry, The Poet's Owl, will be published in October 2022.

Jess Beck (Cox) is a museum professional residing in West Babylon, NY. She writes while juggling her three-year-old human and five- year-old cat. Her poetry focuses heavily on oranges, although she doesn't particularly like the taste, and the ocean although the depths are terrifying.

Antonio Bellia (Madly Loved) A renaissance man. He has traveled many paths. A man of deep sentiment drawn to the performing arts. He has performed as a dancer, actor throughout his lifetime. From a very young age he was compelled to express his emotions and experiences in the form of poetry. They have been shared through his passionate readings in the N.Y. area. Antonio is known by many as Madly Loved.

Robyn Bellospirito is a professional fine artist listed in Who's Who in American Art and Who's Who of American Women. She holds a Bachelor's Degree in Art History and has worked in some of New York's finest museums including The Metropolitan Museum of Art and The Frick Collection. Bellospirito is the author of "Memoirs of a Little Ghost: Selected Writings from 2002-2015", "Unearthly Bequests: A Tetralogy of Tiny Terrors", and numerous feature stories in national and international publications. Several articles written by Bellospirito about shamanism have been published in Sacred Hoop Magazine in the UK. In 2021, Bellospirito designed and published "The Bello Spirito Tarot" along with its accompanying guidebook. Aside from her art and writing, Bellospirito plays wooden flute, hand drums, percussion, tanpura, and is a beginner on acoustic guitar. She is also a butoh dancer, ikebana designer, tarot card reader, and a shamanic healer.

Damien Bettinger practices art, music, poetry, and comedy as inspired by the moon in his mind and the ocean in his heart. He is driven to share in a variety of creative perspectives coming from alternative places and he loves to collaborate with open-minded, like hearted, free handed individuals when ever possible!

Reyna Vasquez Bisono Writing has always drawn Reyna like a moth to a flame, filled her with more metaphors and rhymes than her tongue could ever properly articulate. Born with a voice so loud but lips too quiet. Her writing is a reflection of her journey to stay true to herself while navigating life as a first-generation student, a daughter, a sister, and a friend. Her poetry has been published in several literary magazines, including The Journal of Expressive Writing, IceFloe Press and featured by Nymeria Publishing. She is also the proud author of the published collection of poetry "Random Thoughts Breed Expressive Monologues" available on Amazon. You can find her on Instagram: @ReynaWrites_ .

John A. Brennan comes from County Armagh, Ireland. He left his beloved, sacred green isle many years ago to explore the world and has been island hopping ever since.

Laurel Brett lives in Port Jefferson overlooking the harbor with her husband and her puppy. Kafka. She has dedicated her life to teaching literature to community college students. She published a critical study of postmodern literature and a novel *The Schrödinger Girl*. Her poems have appeared in numerous venues. A life long Long Islander, the land and sea are in her blood.

Richard Bronson is on the faculty in the Department of Obstetrics & Gynecology and the Center for Medical Humanities, Compassionate Care & Bioethics of the Renaissance School of Medicine at Stony Brook University and a member of the Board of the Walt Whitman Birthplace Association. He has won the Poem of the Year Award of the American College of Physicians and was recipient of the *Leonard Tow Humanism in Medicine Award.* Dr. Bronson is currently the Poet Laureate of Suffolk County for 2021-2023.

Carlo Frank Calo, grandson of Sicilian immigrants, husband, father, grandfather, born in East Harlem, grew up in the Bronx projects, retired on Long Island. Enjoys fishing, bicycling, poker, working part-time counseling TBI survivors, babysitting his grandchildren, writing eclectically. Publications: Hippocampus Magazine, The Copperfield Review, High Coupe 2014, Down in the Dirt Magazine, Local Gems Press: Suffolk County Poetry Review 2018, Bards Annual 2017- 2020, No Distance Between Us, Walt Whitman's Bicentennial Poets to Come, We Are Beat-National Beat Poetry Foundation.

Lee grace Cannella, M.A., has used the creative arts to increase quality of life for individuals with special needs. Lee has used poetry, memoir writing, and wheelchair dance with disabled veterans and choreographed sign-language into movement for hearing-impaired students. Writing poetry since her youth, her life experiences find their way into her poetry. Living on Long Island since 1963, has planted her, a city person, into suburban richness.

Shannon Cardinuto resides in Selden, New York. She is new at sharing her poems. Her full time job is a hairstylist and she attends online classes as well. She investigates the paranormal on the side with a local group that has been around for just under twenty years. Her writings are mostly based off those experiences. She writes it from what she felt her soul.

Cate Chirico - lives with her kids and furry friends in the beautiful seaside town of Northport where she is inspired daily .

Anne Cognato writes short stories and poems on Long Island. When she is not writing, she is riding her bicycle thinking about what she will write next. This is her first published piece.

Anne Coen is a retired teacher who has been writing poetry since the 1970's. Her venture into performance poetry began when she accidentally signed the clipboard at an open mic. Publication credits include Bards Annual 2014 through 2021, several PPA Literary Reviews, Thirteen Days of Halloween 2014 and 2015, Poets4Paris, Poets4Haiti, Rhyme and Punishment 2019, and The Hands We Hold - Poems Concerning Breast Cancer.

Marty Cohen's poetry and essays have appeared in periodicals and anthologies in the US, England, and Japan since 1970. His book *A Traveller's Alphabet*, with drawings by Henk Pander, was published by Prescott Street Press. Besides writing and teaching, Cohen spent over 40 years as a manager of not-for-profit & government agencies dedicated to the arts, social services, productivity, and teamwork. He lives in New Hyde Park with his wife, the Rabbi of Temple Tikvah, and their daughter.

Jamie Ann Colangelo, a Christian and mother of twins, authored *The Lion and The Lamb Within* and *From The Father's Heart - A Book of Poems and Suggested Gifts To Inspire, Encourage and Bless Those in Your Circle of Influence*. She's published in *Red Penguin* and various poetry anthologies including *Bards*.

Ed Coletti is a poet widely published internationally and he curates the popular blog "No Money In Poetry." Additionally, Ed is a painter, middling chess player, and blues harmonica player. Raised on Long Island in North Floral Park, he has resided in Santa Rosa, California since 1973. Ed attended Chaminade in Mineola prior to leaving for college.

Lorraine Conlin is the Nassau County Poet Laureate Emeritus (2015-2017) Vice-president of the NCPLS and Events Coordinator for PPA. She hosts Tuesdays at the Bellmore Library for PPA, continues weekly poetry workshops on Zoom since they began during the COVID quarantine and co-moderates for the Long Island Writers Guild. Her poems have been published nationally and internationally in anthologies and literary reviews.

Jane Connelly is an artist and writer who lived in Guam, M.I., before moving to Long Island, NY. She has won numerous awards and has been published in *The Avocet, The Bard's Review, Nassau County Poet Laureate Society Review, Oberon, Performance Poets Anthology*, and most recently in the Walt Whitman Birthplace Association's Anthology *"Covid"*. She is on the Advisory Committee of the *Nassau County Poet Laureate Society*, and a member of *"SIP"/Sisters in Poetry*.

Ushiku Crisafulli is a chef, poet, playwright, actor, performance artist, musician and founder of the OpenMind Collective. His most recent publication "Litany of Varied Experiences" was published by Local Gems Poetry Press in New York and he's currently overseeing their Buzzin Bards project in Manchester, England.

Michele Cuomo grew up in Islip and comes back to Long Island when she can. She lives in Winter Springs, Fl with her husband Paul.

Paula Curci is the Nassau County Poet Laureate (2022-2024). She produces Calliope's Corner - The Place Where Poets and Songwriters Meet & What's the Buzz ® on WRHU.ORG. She co-founded The Acoustic Poets Network ™ and is a retired counselor. Her Posics ™ style poetry is found on streaming services.

Samantha Curra is a dog-loving, coffee-fueled poet who works as a marketing copywriter for Northwell Health, the largest healthcare provider in New York. Her work has been featured in multiple art and literary journals, including *Narrateur, Reflections on Caring* and *Prompt Literary Magazine*, among others. A fanatic for word games, Wordle is her latest obsession.

Jackie Dawn is a writer and editor from Floral Park. She began writing at seven years old, and has since had her work featured in several publications, including *The Writer's Apprentice* at Susquehanna University and *The Inspiration Room* exhibition by HBO. Jackie holds a BA in English with a concentration in creative writing and literature, and has worked as a proof-reader and copy editor for the last 16 years. She lives in Westbury with her cat, Nico, and entirely too many books.

Max Dawson works full-time with adults with mental illness. But Dawson is better defined by his interests in The Civil War, The old west, trains of that era, Victorian science fiction and horror, and most importantly, writing. He has been published in Bard's Annual Poetry Anthology, he has also been published in The Beat Generation Poetry Anthology, and he is writing a book.

Jeanne D'Brant is a physiology and anatomy professor, the author of Global: A Traveler's Tales and an aging but still in-the-game adventurer.

India DeCarmine both lives and works on Long Island. She is a story teller, and has often written biographical poems at the request of friends. Her tendency is to rhyme.

Debbie De Louise is a librarian and the author of the Cobble Cove and Buttercup Bend cozy mystery series. She has also published five standalone novels and a collection of cat poems. Her stories and poetry appear in dozens of anthologies, including the Red Penguin Collection, the Bards Annual, and the Nassau County Voices in Verse. Debbie lives on Long Island with her family and two cats. Learn more about her and her work at:
https://debbiedelouise.com.

Born, raised, and still living in East Meadow, NY, **Ben Diamond** is a songwriter and new age beat poet. Like Charles Baudelaire, Ben writes songs and poems that are quintessentially useless, absolutely innocent, and written with no other aim than to divert himself and to practice his passionate taste for the difficult.

Michael E Dilgen is an aspiring musician and songwriter living in Suffolk County, NY. Naturally, he began writing poetry as a means of developing lyrics as linguistic meaning within song. He finds inspiration in his love of Eastern philosophy as well as his agnosticism and a strong sense of wonder.

Michael Duff was born in Manhattan but even at a young age recognized the rents were ridiculous, and so spent a few years in the Bronx before attending Catholic schools in Queens. He moved on to Michigan State then London City College, which lately has gotten upgraded to London City University, a move diluting its urban charm and one Douglas Adams would condemn if he could. After that he lived in Queens again for a good long time, then Lindenhurst briefly. He has resided in Freeport the past four years playing the Ramones and complaining about the drink prices on the Nautical Mile.

Peter V. Dugan, former Nassau County Poet Laureate, NY (2017-19). He has published several collections of poetry and co-edited four poetry anthologies. He has many awards most notably, being twice nominated for Pushcart Prizes 2016 for his poems: *Jesus Never Rode a Harley* & *Mile 0*, an Honorable Mention by The American Academy of Poets, for *Hey Bobby* (1994).

Madelyn Edelson has always written poetry, even during the 28 years spent teaching English and Humanities at Oceanside Senior High School.

Alex Edwards-Bourdrez's poetry has won prizes and has appeared in various anthologies published on Long Island. Retired from careers in education, public relations, fundraising, and disability services, he is co-manager of a local food pantry, co-chair of the Long Island Alliance of Braver Angels, and a volunteer in various capacities at St. Paul's United Methodist Church in Northport, where he lives with his wife, Susan.

Lynn B. Elfe An Educator for people of all ages, a Mediator of people in all stages, a Mentor of many former students, who have moved forward onto their adult lives. A Writer of education strategies, to keep families away from academic strife, and most importantly, a Poet who can find the words of rhythm and rhyme, for the words that wake me up at any ole time.

Kayla Elfers is finishing her Bachelor's Degree in Creative Writing and Theatre at SUNY Oswego. She recently directed *A Play Where Nothing Happens* by Maizy Broderick Scarpa. Kayla lives on Long Island with her family.

Melissa E. Filippelli is a native Long Islander. She has had a love for words and their meaning since she was a small child. She writes to express her heart and to heal it. Melissa's writing can be found in a number of Bard's Annual publications as well as special projects put out by Local Gems Press and one very special project involving the honorable Walt Whitman.

Adam D Fisher is the author of poetry, stories and liturgy. In addition to publishing many poems in journals and magazines, he has published four books of poetry: *Rooms, Airy Rooms* (Writers Ink, Cross Cultural Communications and Behrman House), *Dancing Alone* (Birnham Wood/ LI Quarterly), *Enough to Stop the Heart* (Writers Ink) and *Hanging Out With God* (Writers Ink.) He was Poetry Editor (2006-2014) of the CCAR Journal, the Journal of the Central Conference of American Rabbis.

Ginamarie Foceri was born and raised in Suffolk County, NY, where she currently resides. She is the author of a novel, White Lies, which is available on Amazon. Ginamarie loves to write poetry, novels, and also enjoys painting.

Rich Follett is a Middle School Theatre Arts teacher who has been writing poems and songs for more than fifty years. He was born and raised on Long Island and moved after college to Virginia, where he has mostly remained. Rich is the poet laureate for Strasburg, Virginia. His poems have been featured in numerous online and print journals, including BlazeVox, the

Montucky Review, the Willows Wept Review, Poetic Diversity, and CounterExample Poetics, for which he is a featured artist. His most recent volume, photo-ku, is available through NightWing Publications. Three volumes of poetry, *Responsorials* (with Constance Stadler), *Silence, Inhabited,* and *Human & c.* are available through NeoPoiesis Press (www.neopoiesispress.com)

John M. Fraioli is a professional brewer who resides in Islip Terrace NY. In June of 2020 he self published his first book of poetry and song lyrics "Thoughts From The Brew Deck". John's poetry has tendencies to focus on longing and loss, but also hope, and perseverance.

William Frank, an author of eight books of poetry, is a man with an amiable façade, a witless disregard for reasonable care and a personal nimbus almost nine feet high. His work has previously appeared in *The Dillydoun Review* and he was a runner-up for the *2008 Discovery/The Boston Review* prize offered by the 92nd Street Y. When not writing poetry, he enjoys long hours of losing at chess, bingeing on 1950's Japanese Cinema, taking naps with Scrambles his cat, summering with the Devil, punching cryptids in the face and Kulning.

Bob Freville is the author of Battering the Stem (Journalstone) and the writer-director of the Berkeley TV cult classic Of Bitches & Hounds. His work has been published by Akashic Books, Creem, Horror Sleaze Trash, and others. His first novel, Drive-Thru, will be released by Solivagant on December 1, 2022.

Nicole Fuschetti is an aspiring Long Island writer who has previously had three poems published in the anthology, Unleashing Satellites, as well as her poem *Ablaze* published in Brief Wilderness Magazine. She works full time as a proposal writer but daydreams about all the worlds between the pages of books. Nicole lives with her husband, Garrett and their son Graham near the beautiful and seemingly enchanted Pine Barrens.

M. Frances Garcia, M.A., is a freelance journalist, poet, and contemplative photographer. She is also and adjunct professor of English at Suffolk Community College, and earned an MSW at Fordham University in Manhattan, NY. She believes in the power of blue lipstick and days spent in nature to heal our hearts.

Tina Lechner Gibbons is a survivor, but her many scars (both inside and out) do not define her. Rather she prefers to think of them as stars in the constellations that have guided her to the place in her life that her soul now inhabits. Tina, who after secretly writing for more than half a century, can now proudly call herself a poet. A poet that has been published on more than one occasion; a poet with an audience for her eclectic, non-conforming, (if sometimes rambling) style, even if the audience may be limited to only one – her work is no longer a secret.

Anthony Gentile is a proud single father of five children. He loves Lord of the Rings, writing and reading.

Martha Gimenez has spent 42 years in and around Brentwood. She has fond memories of the old Entenmann's, the Brentwood Public Library, Sunken Meadow, Captree, and the kindest neighbors you've ever known. She sends warmest wishes to all Long Islanders and readers.

Selena Goetschius a young mom that writes poetry in her free time. A girl that writes a story with a rhyme. A girl that no one knows, but that is working on a talent that shows.

Gloria Gordon photography, poetry and short stories are inspired by her faith in God. Her work has been exhibited at the Creations Art Shows at OSA in NYC. She Attended John J. College.

Paul Thomas Grecco is a poet. He grew up on Long Island. He lives in Astoria, Queens. He is a member of the windbag poetry collective.

Aaron Griffin is an alleged copywriter and novelist who worked full time in a warehouse club outside of Charlotte, NC and now lives in Ohio. Originally from Long Island, NY. Aaron loves trains, pinwheels, windmills, and useless statistics about Japanese cartoon monsters. His favorite activities include spinning things, playing with imaginary animals, shaking things, and watching ice melt.

Valerie Griggs A graduate of the Brooklyn College MFA program (1985), Valerie has been writing and publishing poetry for several decades. Her poems have appeared in publications from the Ledge when it was printed in Timothy Monaghan's Queens basement and stapled together, to the Brooklyn Review, October 2021. Her first poetry book, *Listen and Leap*, published April, 2022 by Words with Wings Press.

George Guida is author of ten books, including five collections of poems, most recently *New York and Other Lovers* (revised edition, Encircle Publications, 2021) and *Zen of Pop* (Long Sky Media, 2020).

Maureen Hadzick- Spisak is a retired Reading and English Teacher, an award-winning poet and author of two poetry books: *A Bite of the Big Apple* and *Yesterday I Was Young.* Her poems have appeared in many anthologies. She enjoys writing about and photographing nature.

Geneva L. Hagar lives in Melville, N.Y. She has a BFA from Stony Brook University. Geneva has published four books of poetry and have been accepted for inclusion in several Long Island anthologies, including the PP 25th Anniversary Literary Review contest winners

Nick Hale is the founder and leader of NoVA Bards and the Northern Virginia Poetry Group. He is a co-founder and the current vice president of the

Bards Initiative, a Long Island based poetry nonprofit. Formerly both a literal and metaphorical hat collector, these days, Nick only collects metaphorical hats. He is a partner, publisher, editor, and author with Local Gems Press and has worked on several anthologies including the best-selling *Sound of Solace.* In addition to writing, editing, and performing poetry, Nick enjoys teaching poetry and has given several seminars, panels, and workshops on various poetic topics. In his own poetry, he often enjoys humor and experimenting with different styles, which may make him seem, at times, like he has yet to find his voice. A former almost-teacher, Nick earned a BA in English and an M.Ed in Secondary Education before deciding he didn't want to teach, teaching himself the basics of IT and web design, and then doing neither of those things. Along with James P. Wagner, Nick co-authored *Japanese Poetry Forms: A Poet's Guide.* He is the author of *Broken Reflections* and three upcoming chapbooks which, he claims haven't been published yet only because he's too busy working on books that are not his.

J. Peter Hansen is the founder of both PAL - Poets & Lyricists of Long Island and SLI - the Songwriters of Long Island Facebook groups. He is also a Board Member of the Long Island Blues Society. J. Peter holds a Masters Degree in Music Education and has been an educator since 1985.

Robert L. Harrison has been employed as a Hot Walker, Bouncer, Air Policeman, Photosphere, Special Education Teacher, Dispatcher, Communications Manager, Parking Lot Attendant, docent, Gas Station Attendant, Airplane-Mate Cleaner and Archive worker.

Damian Ward Hey is published in *The RavensPerch, e·ratio, Neologism, Trouvaille Review,* and in an array of other journals and anthologies. He is the founding editor of *Stone Poetry Journal* stonepoetryjournal.com (now *Stone Poetry Quarterly*) and is a professor of literature at Molloy University.

William Heyen (b. 1940) was raised in Nesconset, graduated from Smithtown High School. He is the author or editor of more than 40 books, including

Long Island Light and the National Book Award Finalist collection Shoah Train. In 2021 Mammoth Books published his Nature: Selected & New Poems 1970-2020.

Sheila Hoffenberg has been published in a POETRY ANTHOLOGY 1983, the PPA 2016, 2019, and 2021, NCPL 2018, and 2019 and 2020, BARDS 2019 , PRINCESS RONKONKOMA 2019 and Suffolk Poetry Review 2020. Featured reader at the Levittown Library and Sip This 2019 and a member of the LIWG since 2012.

Arnold Hollander published a quarterly magazine, *Grassroot Reflections* until a pandemic turned the world upside down. His poems can be found in various anthologies: A Budding Joy, The Best Poets of 2007, Towards Forgiveness, Rhyme and PUNishment, and Paumanok Interwoven.   He has poems and short stories in the online magazine, *Bewildering Stories* and keeps a blog at www.arnieh.webs.com.

Kevin Holmes. Poet. Brooklyn and Long Island. Reflector. Family guy.

Larry Jaffe For his entire professional career, Larry Jaffe has been using his art to promote human rights. He was Poet-In-Residence at the Autry Museum of Western Heritage, a featured poet in Chrysler's Spirit in the Words poetry program, co-founder of Poets for Peace (now Poets without Borders), helped spearhead the United Nations Dialogue among Civilizations through Poetry project with hundreds of readings globally using the aesthetic power of poetry to bring understanding to the world, former Poet Laureate Youth for Human Rights and the Florida Beat Poet Laureate. He was the recipient of the Saint Hill Art Festival's Lifetime of Creativity Award. . He has six books of poetry: *Unprotected Poetry, Anguish of the Blacksmith's Forge, One Child Sold, In Plain View, 30 Aught 4, Sirens* and *Man without Borders.*

Gloria Jainchill grew up on Long Island and began writing poetry at age 7 when she "played school" with her ill younger brother. This began a lifelong love of poetry reading and writing. Together they filled 3 volumes of hard covered red books with small sparkling dots, and a hundred blank pages. Gloria has self-published several poetry books, her proudest work being, *Poetry*

Is Fun. Co-authored with her granddaughter to help Amber process her grief when her elementary school closed in 2018.

Alma Johnson loves to write and has been attempting to write different pieces over the years. Her dream which is on her bucket list is to write a book about her life story. She has given it thoughts upon thoughts but has never settled down to begin because she is busy with other activities in life. She already has a title but need to sit down and let her thoughts flow to paper.

Alyssa Johnson is a young adult who has a passion for writing. One of her dreams is to write children's books. She does a great deal of personal writing. She welcomes opportunities where she can improve her writing.

Ryan Jones began writing at an early age and believes it to be the best way to express one's thoughts and ideas. Ryan's topics of interest include nature, human and natural history, mythology, and personal and collective experience, all of which are influential to his writings. Ryan holds a bachelor's degree in English with a master's degree in childhood education, and has worked with children by profession.

Sara Jones has been a poet and an artist all her life. She made the rounds in the NYC poetry scene of the 1970's, opening for Patti Smith at the Village Gate. She appears in the documentary " The Art of the Prank" where she was a regular performer with the political street rep company of Joey Skaggs. Born in Brooklyn, raised on the south shore and now retired to the North Fork of Long Island, Sara is a native New Yorker.

Edward Kenny is an author, lyricist and librettist. He has published several books of poetry and lyrics, including "Bluebird Songs Volumes I and II" and "Lonesome Man on a Hermit's Hill - A Verse Play." He has written the book and lyrics for 10 musicals, including one that was selected as a finalist in the New York Drama League's Grants Competition, along with over 1,300 lyrics.

Daniel Basil Kerr, CPA, Ph.D. is a cross-cultural consultant focused on helping people and organizations be more inclusive and work more effectively across borders. He teaches accounting at St. Joseph's College and Suffolk Community College. Dan is the moderator of the monthly All Souls Church *Second Saturdays* poetry reading. His poems about religion, politics, history, and "growing up in Asharoken in the 1960s" have been published in *Bards Annual, Suffolk County Poetry Review, Performance Poets Association, Beat Generation*, Paumanok, and other anthologies.

Mindy Kronenberg is a widely published poet, writer, and professor of writing and the arts at Empire State College. She edits *Oberon* poetry magazine and is on the editorial board of *Paumanok:* Transition.

Joan F. Kuchner, Ph.D. Ret. Director., Child & Family Studies, Psych. Dept., Stony Brook Univ. honored for her teaching in the fields of infancy, children's play & intergenerational issues, now enjoys writing poetry on these same themes as well as spending time playing with her grandchildren. Her poems have been published in *Lilith, Oberon Poetry Magazine, Bards Annual*, and the *Nassau County Poetry Laureate Society Review.*

Tara Lamberti believes in the power of magic and hopes to spread some of it through her poetry. She has been featured in *Oberon*, previous Bards Annual anthologies, and thanks to a poetic memoir challenge, has a chapbook *Memories of Mastic* published with Local Gems Press.

Billy Lamont is a multimedia poetry performer who has performed on national television a number of times, including MTV and Joe Franklin Show, toured and performed with rock festivals such as Lollapalooza, and appeared on major radio stations across the U.S. He has three books of poetry and nine album CD/digital download releases. His latest book *Words Ripped From A Soul Still Bleeding: Poems For The Future Edition* is available at Barnes And Noble and Amazon as a paperback, or as an eBook, and all his albums can be streamed on Spotify and Apple Music.

Linda Leff Although quietly writing poetry for many years, inclusion in *Bards Annual 2020* has invigorated her passions. Highly motivated to pursue this calling, inspiration can be found in enjoyable moments with family and friends: hikes, archery, fishing or the sights and smells of the seashore. Looking forward to continued participation within Long Island's poetry community.

Nya Devereaux née Masonya is a 35+ year old, retired, psychiatric medical professional. Nya is a proud, Brooklyn native, and twice divorced (by choice), former good girl. She is also an avid fan of naps, paid bills, and traveling. She currently resides in Long Island with her partner, 5 children and animals. You can catch up with her on Instagram: @thedivinecomfycouch

Iris Levin, a retired educator, now works as a photo archivist for Nassau County. She writes with open eyes and open heart seeing her poetry as snapshots of life. She has been published in online and print anthologies. Iris has been awarded honorable mention in the 2020 and 2021 Nassau Poet Laureate Society Review.

Elise Levitt studied creative writing with a concentration in poetry at Hofstra University. She is also a singer songwriter currently living in Astoria, NY. Elise Levitt is excited to publish her writing with the Bards Initiative

Janine Logan is a native Long Islander who grew up on the south shore near the Great South Bay. The mother of four grown children, she continues to chronicle the lives of her children through essays, blogs posts, and more recently, poetry. A proponent of the narrative approach even for business writing, she specializes in health communications that place the person at the center of the story. She is currently vice president of communications and population health for the Nassau-Suffolk Hospital Council and an adjunct assistant professor of community health at Farmingdale State College.

Once business/tech innovator, now award-winning poet and photographer **Sheri Lynn**, 2018-2022, was published by: *Ms. Magazine, Long Island Quarterly, Chicken Soup for the Soul Listen to Your Dreams, Paumanok Transitions* (co-editor), Bard's, *NCPLS, PPA, DBP, TNSPS, 911 Memorial Museum, Poets4Haiti, LIWG's The Odyssey and more.* In 2019 she launched her debut chapbook *Nature's Breath*, accompanying notecards and BreatheInsights.com. Sheri is a LIWG, LIPC and LIAG member and UUCSR's Poetry weekly discussion co-facilitator. She is grateful to family, friends, and the writing community for encouragement in this transformative and exciting artistic journey!

John Lysaght is a poet who began honing his craft while at university graduating in 1968 with a degree in English and Classics. He holds a Masters in Social Work degree and a private investigator's license. This spring his chapbook, Naturescapes, will debut from Kelsay Press.

Mikayla Lyston is a poet from Long Island, NY. Mikayla has made appearances in the Albertus Magnus College art magazine "Breakwater" at her school- Albertus Magnus College. Mikayla Lyston is 21 years old and aspires to develop her craft as a poet. One of Mikayla's favorite poets is Emily Dickinson.

Joan Magiet is a former Assistant Professor of English, adjunct faculty at SUNY, Nassau, N.Y., an award winning magazine article writer, journalist and poet. She is a founding member of PPA, former contest judge and editor. She is the author of four books of poetry. "Tender Chains" and "Haiku For Jewtalian Mothers" are available on Amazon under her pen name, Joan Beverly.

Nicholas Malerba is 8 years old and has been writing poetry for several years. Nicholas loves exploring nature and writing about his observations and ways we can help our planet.

Cristian Martinez is a 15-year-old 10th-grade student at Connetquot School and award-winning poet. He has been published in over 15 published anthologies throughout the years. He was awarded for his poem, "Glimpse of Tomorrow" with recognition as the Grand Champion for the Walt Whitman Birthplace Contest and published in their anthology in 2019. *Glimpse of Tomorrow* is Cristian's first book that has now been published in 2021. He has been mentored by Robert Savino which has helped Cristian fine-tune his craft. Cristian also loves to play soccer.

Michael McCarthy resides in East Northport with his wife, Toni Ann. Now retired, he is eager to spend more time with his two grandchildren. He had taught theology courses on social justice and loss, grief, & healing at the Mary Louis Academy for the past sixteen years. Michael is a lifetime explorer of the sacred and author of The Ways of Grace: A Book of Poems (published by Goldfinch Publishing in 2016).

Rosemary McKinley The author is a Long Island girl through and through, who finds herself near water often. Her poetry has been published in Lucidity, Clarity, canvasli.com, and the wormwood press.com. www.rosemarymckinley.com

Janet McLaren-Wade, (BSc Management Studies) (MSc Accounting) lives in Nassau County,she has been attending and partici- pating various locations featured and in their open mike sessions. McLaren-Wade poetry is wide based and has been written to inspire and motivate individuals from a spiritual point of view. Each of her poems expresses her devotion to God and show how He has used the challenges in her life to shape and refine her way of thinking. Her poem Ship- wreck was awarded (3rd place) at the Bard's Super Poem Contest in 2017.

Gene McParland (North Babylon, NY): A graduate from Queens College and possessing graduate degrees from other institutions, Gene has published various research papers *BUT* have always had a passion for poetry and the messages it can convey. His works have appeared in numerous publications, and previous editions of the Bards Annual. He is also the author of Baby Boomer Ramblings, a collection of essays and poetry, and Adult Without, Child Within, poetry celebrating our inner child. Gene also performs in Community Theater and film, mostly home grown original works; and has written several plays.

Ria Meade A native Long Islander, Ria Meade crafts poems about her adult life as a blind woman. Painting since childhood, her passion culminated with a degree in fine arts. Twenty-five years after losing her sight, she began to paint again with words. Ria has recently completed her sixth self-published collection. She survives this vulnerable existence independently with her beloved 8th guide dog and many newly discovered senses.

Alice Melzer is a writer, artist, and educator. Her poetry is included in several anthologies. When not working she can be found finding shells along real and imagined beaches or hiking in other outdoor locations throughout and beyond Long Island's boarders.

Lisa Diaz Meyer ALL ROADS HOME, ALL ROADS DESTINED, and ALL ROADS SHATTERED are New York author, Lisa Diaz Meyer's current works of multi-genre dark fiction and poetry. Readers can also find her short stories and poetry in several anthologies published by Red Penguin Books, Nassau County Voices In Verse, and Bards Annual. For more info visit lisadiazmeyer.com

Rita Monte Upon her arrival to America from Italy at age 12; Rita Monte wrote her very first poem, and has won numerous poetry contests ever since. She has read her work at several poetry venues as well. Her poems have been featured in some literary magazines, and published in the Nassau County Poet Laureate Society Review, Bards Annual Poetry Anthology and No Distance between Us, Italian American Poets of Long Island.

CR Montoya publishes children's stories, featuring *Papa The Happy Snowman*. He published a short story titled *Return to Bedford Falls* in January 2022. Based on the movie *It's A Wonderful Life*, the story carries readers through time describing how the lives of the movies glorious characters evolved after that fateful Christmas Eve. All his stories can be found on Amazon.

Glenn Murphy is a lifelong resident of Long Island who enjoys the beauty, the pace, and the people of the Island who have helped shape his life. He holds a Bachelor of Science degree in business administration from Marist College and was involved in both the telecommunications and vertical transportation industries. Glenn's hobbies include writing poetry, the New York Rangers, and a cold beer with warm friends.

Edward Nardoza is an editor and writer based in Hampton Bays, L.I. He has contributed to various international publications, most recently serving as Editor in Chief of Penske Media's WWD.

Valerie Nifora was raised in New York to Greek immigrant parents. She credits her Greek heritage for her love of words and storytelling. Her collection of romantic poetry, *I Asked the Wind* won several awards. Her first romance novel, *The Fairmounts,* a historical romantic-suspense story, debuted as a #1 New Release on Amazon. Her works call forth a time of leather-bound books and soft comfortable chairs drawn close to the warmth of a hearth. Valerie holds a B.A. in Communications from Emerson College and an M.B.A. from Fordham University. She is married and a mother of two amazing sons.

George H. Northrup is a poet and psychologist in New Hyde Park, NY. He is the author of *You Might Fall In* (2014), *Wave into Wave, Light into Light: Poems and Places* (2019), *When Sunset Weeps: Homage to Emily Dickinson* (2020), and *Old Caterpillar* (2021).

Mark C. Nuccio has been a Long Island Poet for 40 Years. He has five chap book collections and contributed to the recent collection "No Distance Between Us," Honoring the 700th year of Dantes Birth. He has contributed to Poetry Bay, Fire Island Tides, Fire Island News, Long Island Traditions, Long Island Boating, The Amityville Record, Babylon Beacon and other venues. Mark is a Trustee of the Walt Whitman Birthplace in Melville, Long Island.

Gracie Conway Panousis *is a poet and essayist whose writing has appeared in The New York Times, the English Journal and several poetry anthologies.*

Marlene Patti is a Chilean born poet who resides in Selden, NY with her husband, two sons, a corgi and a Guinea pig. Marlene is a Licensed Real Estate Salesperson and a student at Stony Brook University in the Master's of Social Work program. She is passionate about humans rights and living life to the fullest! Find her on IG @marlene.is.key.

Mary C. M. Phillips is a caffeinated wife, mom, writer and musician. Her work has been published in numerous bestselling inspirational anthologies. Her spoken-word poetry is available via streaming platforms such as Spotify and Pandora. Follow her on twitter @marycmphil.

Kelly Powell is a poet from Long Island.

Dr. **Pearl Ketover Prilik** is a poet/writer/psychoanalyst, who believes poetry captures life in a way that eludes linear language. Her writing is varied including several nonfiction books, stints as editor of a post-doc psychoanalytic newsletter and editor/participant of two international poetry journals. PKP has been writing poetry since early childhood and is widely published. Living on a barrier island on the south shore of Long Island, NY with DJ, her husband extraordinaire and Oliver, the humanoid cat, she continues to write because she simply has no other choice in the matter. More on PKP at "Imagine" http://drpkp.com

Alexander Radison is a PhD candidate in English at St. John's University. In 2018, he received his MFA in creative writing from Queens College, with a focus on poetry. He currently teaches English and creative writing Farmingdale State College. His creative work has appeared in *Newtown Literary, The Violet Hour, The Coachella Review*, and *Rattle*, among other publications.

Phil Reinstein {aka Insurance Mon} is a poet and musician plying his poems and music at various cafes and libraries and bars around Long Island.

Diana R. Richman, Ph.D. licensed psychologist, has been in private practice for several decades. Listening to stories shared by souls, authoring self-help publications, writing rhymes for special occasions since childhood, and playing the cello in community orchestras evoked the desire to express her soul's voice through the musical language of poetry.

Allie Rieger has lived on Long Island her whole life. She lives with her fiancé and their cat. Typically she can be found watching a horror movie, working on her writing or attempting to paint. She has multiple poems published with bards and a few other publications, and looks forward to publishing more!

John Robilotta resides in Sayville. He has been involved in the local poetry scene for many years going back to readings at Runaway Bay bookstore. He has also done readings at American Cheese Shop. During the winter, he resides in Ft. Myers, Florida, where he is a member of the Poetry Alliance, part of the Alliance for the Arts. He is excited to attend readings and open mikes this summer at The Dog-Eared Bards Book Shop.

Rita B. Rose is a published author, poet and playwright. To date, she is Long Island's LGBTQ poet laureate. Her poems have appeared in various anthologies abroad and in the United States of America. She is the author of *Flower Poems: Personalties In bloom.*

Patricia Rossi For over a decade Patricia has facilitated weekly "writing to heal" workshops for cancer survivors. Patricia has also created and implemented numerous empowerment writing workshops for females residing in under-served communities. She also runs a weekly writing club for developmentally and intellectually disabled adults.

Noted Vogon poetry champion **A. A. Rubin** has been accosting people with his poetry for years. His work has appeared recently in The Deronda Review, Love Letters to Poe, and Nassau County Voices in Verse. He can be reached on social media as @TheSurrealAri, or through his website, www.aarubin.com.

Brion Ryder, born among row houses of Brooklyn, now residing along sand lined coasts of Suffolk County, has held Long Island as the only home he has ever known. The husband of a rock star wife he is a member of a extremely underrated band, in his estimations. He does his best writing wandering forgotten trails and while driving along the Long Island Expressway. While the latter is far more dangerous it seems to inspire his best work.

Pat Gallagher Sassone's poetry was published in NASTY WOMEN POETS and Local Gems' CHAOS A POETRY VORTEX and, TREES IN A GARDEN OF ASHES. A longtime resident of Floral Park and Southold, her poetry often reflects an intimate connection with the sea, Long Island's greatest gift to her.

Robert Savino, Suffolk County Poet Laureate 2015-2017, is a native Long Island poet, Board Member at the Walt Whitman Birthplace and Long Island Poetry & Literature Repository Center. He is the winner of the 2008 Oberon Poetry Prize. Robert is co-editor of two bilingual collections of Italian Americans Poets, *No Distance Between Us - Italian American Poets*. His books include *fireballs of an illuminated scarecrow, Inside a Turtle Shell* and *I'm Not the Only One Here*. He currently enjoys his role as poetry mentor.

Karen Schulte is a retired social worker and therapist who began writing in grade school and, since retirement, has had her poetry published in a number of journals and anthologies including, Long Island Quarterly, 25th Anniversary Edition, Poetica Magazine, Paterson Review, Bards Annual, PPA Literary Review, NCPL Literary Review. Her collection of poetry, "Where Desire Settles," won first place in the Writer's Digest 2017 Annual Contest for a self-published book of poetry. Her chapbook, "Black Paper Album," will be published by Finishing Line Press in early 2023.

Sophia Schiralli is a poet and writer from Long Island. She works as an editor and script writer for a military channel, and is an Army Veteran. She loves Russian Literature, her poetry, and is fascinated by neurolinguistics and psychology.

Jacqueline Shortell-McSweeney writes only when inspired, or when her Muse, Noreen, stands over her with a metaphorical rolling pin. At other times, she has worked as a producer for Women Make Movies (Where WHY WOMEN STAY was produced and directed.), a video artist at Henry St., Settlement, first union woman grip on the East Coast, and then, as a lawyer, in hopes she could sue some of those responsible for her Me-Too moments in the union. Finally, as an attorney for Women's Venture Fund, Ms. Shortell-McSweeney worked with women entrepreneurs to help build their businesses. Now retired to her writing desk, Shortell-McSweeney has been published in eight anthologies, the latest being BEAT GENERATION. Her detective story, DR. ALTMAN AND THE CONCUBINES, is recently published and in bookstores. Now, The Muse wants to see her continue with her poetry and thriller, THE PLAYGIRL MURDERS. Most important, she is to spend precious time with her loving family.

Keith A Simmons, a Long Island native, has performed poetry for over 20 years. He holds a deep appreciation of nature, adventure and alternate perspectives. Humor, absurdity, activism, compassion and spirituality weave their way into his poems, haiku, short stories and songs.

Leslie Simon is a published poet and a retired elementary school teacher, excelling in computer instruction and poetry, she is also the recipient of prestigious poetry awards. In addition, she is an avid quilter for which she has combined this art form with poetry in her book *Pieces of My Heart*. It is a unique poetry book, in that each poem is illustrated by a corresponding quilt. The quilts tell the story of the poems.

Emily-Sue Sloane (emilysuesloane.com) is an award-winning Huntington Station-based poet who writes to capture moments of wonder, worry and human connection. She is the author of a full-length poetry collection, *We Are Beach Glass* (2022), and her poems have appeared in a variety of journals and anthologies.

Lynne D. Soulagnet has been published in The Avocet, Amethyst Review [UK], Paumanok Transitions, and many others. She writes about her deep affection for the natural world, and about human nature which she finds both fascinating and bewildering at times. She is active in poetry venues on Long Island.

Ivy Sommer A widow with two young boys, Ivy Sommer used the love of her children to help fuel her passion for poetry while struggling with the loss of her husband after a multi-year struggle with a terminal disease. Ivy's poems run the gamut of emotions from whimsical to reflective, childlike to melancholy. Ivy Sommer has lived in Dix Hills for 32 years.

Doreen (Dd.) Spungin, author of the collection, *Tomorrow Smells Invisible,* hosts for Poets In Nassau and PPA. Her poetry can be found in anthologies and in print and on-line journals, most recently L I Quarterly, Maintenant 16, First Literary Review East, Poets To Come, Paumonok~Transition and Corona, An Anthology of Poems.

Ed Stever, *Bards Laureate 2015-2017* Poet, playwright, actor, and director, he has published two collections of poetry with Writers Ink Press:

Transparency and *Propulsion. The Man with Tall Skin*, was published by Local Gems Press in December of 2014. In that same year he compiled and edited *Unleashing Satellites: The Undergrad Poetry Project.* He recently took first place in the Village of Great Neck Plaza's 5th Annual Poetry Contest. He is one of the editors of the *Suffolk County Poetry Review.*

d w Stojek is a poet, photographer and general nuisance to those within earshot. He is eagerly awaiting the day when 'Build-a-Bear' re-opens as a series of genetic labs along the coast of the very fictional Luneville. He spends life happily in company of his beloved Bunny, Biscuits and Munchkin, along with the bestest of friends: Cucujid. His volume of poetry entitled " a dark woods' summation' will soon be available.

Lennon Stravato A native Long Islander, Lennon Stravato is a screenwriter, lyricist, poet, and former Foreign Policy Contributor for The Hill newspaper in Washington D.C.

Jaishree Subramani is a physician in Internal and Occupational medicine and likes to dabble in poetry. Her other interests include reading,music, art and tennis.

Douglas G. Swezey received his B.A. in English and Art History from Stony Brook University in 2004, has written as a journalist for many weekly newspapers, was Managing Editor of *Government Food Services Magazine* and author of *Stony Brook University: Off The Record* (College Prowler, 2005). He currently serves on the Board of Directors for the Bards Initiative, Long Island Poetry Collective, and, formerly, the North Sea Poetry Scene. He is the host of the First Fridays Reading Series at the Dog-Eared Bard's Book Shop and co-creator of Super Poem Sunday.

James Tucker is a retired firefighter from the FDNY residing in Wantagh LI. with loving family. He enjoys time with friends, playing guitar and writing poetry.

J R (Judy) Turek, Superintendent of Poetry for the LI Fair, 2020 Hometown Hero by the *East Meadow Herald,* 2019 LI Poet of the Year, NYS 2017 Woman of Distinction, Bards Laureate 2013-2015, 25 years as Moderator of the Farmingdale Creative Writing Group; two Pushcart nominations, recipient of the Conklin Prize for Poetry; editor, workshop leader, and author of six poetry books, the most recent *24 in 24.* 'The Purple Poet' has written a poem a day for over 18 years; she lives on Long Island with her soul-mate husband, Paul, her dogs, and her extraordinarily extensive shoe collection. msjevus@optonline.net

Victoria Twomey is a poet and an artist. She has appeared as a featured poet at venues around Long Island, including The Poetry Barn, Barnes & Noble, and Borders Books. Her poems have been published in several anthologies, in newspapers and on the web, including Sanctuary Magazine, BigCityLit, Long Island Quarterly, Autumn Sky Poetry Daily, The Tipton Poetry Journal, Verse-Virtual, The Agape Review and The Trouvaille Review. Her poem "Pieta" was nominated for a Pushcart Prize.

James P. Wagner (Ishwa) is an editor, publisher, award-winning fiction writer, essayist, historian, actor, comedian, performance poet, and alum twice over (BA & MALS) of Dowling College. He is the publisher for Local Gems Poetry Press and the Senior Founder and President of the Bards Initiative. He is also the founder and Grand Laureate of Bards Against Hunger, a series of poetry readings and anthologies dedicated to gathering food for local pantries that operates in over a dozen states. His most recent individual collection of poetry is *Everyday Alchemy.* He was the Long Island, NY National Beat Poet Laureate from 2017-2019. He was the Walt Whitman Bicentennial Convention Chairman and has taught poetry workshops at the Walt Whitman Birthplace State Historic Site. James has edited over 100 poetry anthologies and hosted book launch events up and down the East Coast. He was named the National Beat Poet Laureate of the United States from 2020-2021. He is the owner/operator of The Dog-Eared Bard's Book Shop in East Northport, New York.

Jillian Wagner earned her BA in Creative Writing from Dowling College. She is an active member of Fanfiction.net and just released her collection of short stories entitled *13 Dark Tales*. She was one of the founding editors of *Conspiracy*, a genre fiction magazine at Dowling College. She is a certified paralegal and sits on the board for the Bards Initiative. She currently helps operate The Dog-Eared Bard's Book Shop.

Margarette Wahl, Special Ed Teacher Aide, Poet from Massapequa,Long Island. She is published in a number of Anthologies and has four chapbooks with Local Gems Press. Her poem is dedicated to her classmate Frankie who walked into her Health Class in 1988 and changed her life forever.

Herb Wahlsteen earned a B.A. in English from CA. St. U., Fullerton, and an M. A. in English from Columbia U. He then worked many years as a high-school teacher in New York City Public Schools. He was a finalist in the Yale Series of Younger Poets contest (1989, Adam and Eve in the 20th Century, James Merrill, judge), placed 3rd in the Writer's Digest 77th Annual Writing Competition: Rhyming Category, and has had poems published in: Long Island Quarterly, the Great South Bay Magazine, The Long Islander, The Lyric magazine, Paumanok Interwoven and Transitions, Suffolk County Poetry Review, Bards Annual, Form Quarterly, Bards Against Hunger, 13 Days of Halloween, Poets to Come, The Hands We Hold, A Tree in a Garden of Ashes, Beat Poets Anthology, String Poet (2 poems translated from the French, 2 poems translated from the Spanish), Pratik; A Magazine of Contemporary Writing, and Measure magazine.

George Wallace is writer in residence at the Walt Whitman Birthplace, first poet laureate of Suffolk County, and author of 38 chapbooks of poetry. A native of Long Island and New York City, he travels worldwide to share his poetry.

Virginia Walker, Ph.D. taught writing and literature courses at New England and Long Island colleges. On Shelter Island, she acted as facilitator for the Art/Rich Poetry Roundtable and has curated four Webinars on poets and poetry for the Shelter Island Library. She is the co-author of the poetry book *Neuron Mirror* (with Michael Walsh) which raised over $10,700 for the Lustgarten Foundation for pancreatic cancer research. Her poems have appeared in *Nassau Review, Minetta Review, Light of City and Sea, Touched by Eros, Bards Annual, Poets 4 Paris, Suffolk County Poetry Review*, and the *Humanist*.

Lorraine Wodhanil Retired high school library asst. responsible for organizing student poetry slams as well as author and illustrator visits

Jack Zaffos has been writing poetry since he was 18 years old. After retirement he made a commitment to get his work out to the public. He is the Calendar Coordinator for PPA. He has three books published ***Meditations Of The Heart, Songlines In The Wilderness*** and ***Lyrics From A Singing Stream.***

Steven Zaluski is a long Island artist and SUNY Stony Brook graduate, class of 1974. He creates metal sculpture, that is collected around the world, and loves to paint, write, create music and video, improvise performance art, swim in the ocean, bays and lakes, and enjoy life wherever he travels...

Thomas Zampino, a New York City attorney for over 35 years, started writing poetry only recently (https://thomaszampino.wordpress.com). Some of his works have appeared in The University of Chicago's *Memoryhouse Magazine, Silver Birch Press* (twice)*, Bard's Annual 2019, 2020, and 2021, Trees in a Garden of Ashes, Otherwise Engaged, Chaos, A Poetry Vortex, Nassau County Voices in Verse*, and *No Distance Between Us*. A video enactment of his poem *Precise Moment* was produced by Brazilian director and actor Gui Agustini. His first book of poetry, *Precise Moment*, was published in August 2021.

A multi-purpose poetry project, The Bards Initiative is dedicated to connecting poetry communities, while promoting the writing and performance of poetry. The Initiative provides avenues for poets to share their work and encourages the use of poetry for social change.

In addition, the Initiative aims to make use of modern technologies to help spread poetry and encourage and inspire poetry, particularly in the younger generations. It is the core belief of the Bards Initiative that poetry is the voice of the people and can be used to help create a sense of sharing and community.

www.bardsinitiative.weebly.com

Local Gems Poetry Press is a small Long Island based poetry press dedicated to spreading poetry through performance and the written word. Local Gems believes that poetry is the voice of the people, and as the sister organization of the Bards Initiative, believes that poetry can be used to make a difference.

www.localgemspoetrypress.com

Made in the USA
Middletown, DE
02 October 2022

11609109R00159